BOYS TALK ABOUT GIRLS, GIRLS TALK ABOUT BOYS

BOYS TALK ABOUT GIRLS,
GIRLS TALK ABOUT BOYS

Judi Miller

SCHOLASTIC INC.
New York Toronto London Auckland Sydney

ISBN 0-590-31585-4

Copyright © 1981 by Judi Miller. All rights reserved. Published by Scholastic Inc.

12 11 10 9 8 7 6 5 4 3 2   8 9/8 0 1 2 3/9

Printed in the U.S.A.   01

CONTENTS

INTRODUCTION

This book is a collection of what real boys and girls, just like you and your friends, have to say. They talk about how it feels to meet someone at a dance and suddenly find no words are coming out of a throat as dry as the Sahara Desert; how awkward it is to break up with someone one night and then have to sit next to that person in class the next day; or how good it feels to find a truly best friend of the opposite sex. And more!

Girls, find out what boys are talking about. Boys, find out what girls are saying.

Boys
Talk
About
Girls

THE GIRL OF MY DREAMS

Too corny for words? But it's true. Just like those old-fashioned records straight from the nostalgia hour, boys of today do have a girl of their dreams. A certain special type that attracts them. She might look like a goddess or a gypsy. But one special girl will stand out and be the only one a boy will see. That's the girl he's dreaming about, consciously or unconsciously, and that's the girl he will try to meet.

This first attraction involves "chemistry." It's sometimes harder to understand than the course in school, by the same name, offered in 11th or 12th grade. Chemistry is what makes a boy attracted to a girl, without even really knowing her. Sometimes a girl wonders about this. Why doesn't the boy *she* likes ever talk to her? Why are his eyes floating over his book to catch every move of a girl who's not even as pretty? It's chemistry. Some people call it "vibes." And no one knows why. Except that you feel the same way about a boy *you* find attractive, don't you?

What is it boys like in girls, at first glance? What kind of girl would they go up to and start talking to?

Kevin, 16, anwers rather bluntly:

> "What attracts me first about a girl? Looks. Mainly, good-looking girls."

Pete, 15, agrees:

"Right off? Her looks. After that it could go either way. Sometimes it could be her figure or sometimes her personality. It depends on how well I know her. For first impressions, though, first off, you think of looks."

As long as boys like girls and girls like boys, and men like women and women like men, this is one of the cruel facts about socializing. Each sex tends to look for appearance first.

Gee, thanks, you're probably saying. Where does that leave you? But the secret of looking attractive, is to look like a person other people would want to meet or know. It doesn't take anything as drastic as plastic surgery, a body transplant, or a fairy godmother to do the trick.

Carl, 13, says of the type of girl he would go up to and try to meet:

"Attractive girls catch my eye. Always. I don't like chubby girls, not that I'm the skinniest person in the world. I like girls with clean faces, not a lot of make-up."

Looking nice comes back to packaging yourself attractively. It's so simple to do. You need a clean complexion; hair that's cut just right for you and is always in good condition; and clothes that fit well and look good.

It may mean eating oranges instead of cake for lunch. Unfortunately. It also means not being obsessed by the part of you that can't be changed (height, shoe size, pointy elbows) and changing the part that can be changed (weight, hairstyle, skin).

Hoping for picture-perfect looks in the form of an overnight miracle is so easy to slip into, but it's such a waste of time. Work with what you have. It's probably more than you think.

Here's a simple checklist you can follow for looking good. Answer honestly and go on to make your own list of what *you* have to do to look your best.

1. Hair. Is it cut right? Is it conditioned? Is it clean? Does it sparkle with good health?

2. Weight. Do you need to gain? Should you lose? Maybe you have to make maintaining (don't gain, don't lose) your weight your goal.

3. Complexion. Too many pimples and blemishes? Do you need to take your babysitting money and spend it on a dermatologist (skin doctor)? Is your skin too dry? Can you find your skin under all the makeup?

4. Clothes. Do you wear clothes that look terrific on you or better on the other girls who are all wearing the same thing? Do you know you look sick in olive green but sensational in cherry red? Are your clothes wrinkle-free, dirt-free, cling- or droop-free? Do they make you feel good about yourself?

5. Have you mastered the easiest beauty trick of all? The secret of movie stars and some of the girls in your school that seem to be so popular? That secret is working just as hard on the inside of yourself as you do on the outside.

Not all boys are drawn to good-looking girls as an absolute First Attraction. Even Kevin and Pete, after being questioned, had to admit they look for other qualities in a girl as well. Let's go back to them.

Kevin's second thought:

> "I have a special type — the intelligent, hardworking, good-looking girl. I like intelligent girls. I guess I could sacrifice some of the looks."

(Notice how good-looking got bumped to third place. It was in first place before he started to *really* think about what he liked in girls.)

Pete admits to this after-thought:

> "Oh, I couldn't go for an 'airhead.' No matter how nice looking. First, I'm attracted to looks. Right from there, I go on to see how we react together."

It all amounts to this: Once we get underneath that packaging that attracts a boy and makes him want to come up and say something like, "Hi, wanna dance?" there's more than meets the eye. After he sizes up what you're like, sometimes in the space of five minutes or less, it doesn't matter if you're the most gorgeous creature in the world, if there's nothing inside your head or heart, your looks won't do you any good.

Brian, 14, does not even put looks at the top of his list:

"It has a lot to do with personality. If she's vibrant and full of life. Not somebody who's really dull to be around. Somebody that has a lot of depth to her personality."

However, looks can mean many things and they mean something different to Joe:

"I have to say I don't look for the 'perfect person.' Like the 'in' model or TV star. I don't like that. I like the 'different' look. Certain things about the face, say, that might be different from most other people."

Richie, 15, doesn't look for looks at all:

"She doesn't have to be pretty. Usually I listen to her speaking to someone else for a while just to get an idea of what she's like, what kind of person she is. Then I go up and talk to her."

So if you fantasize endlessly about being the kind of breathtakingly beautiful girl all boys can't resist, can't get a date with . . . forget it! Not every boy would go for you, anyway. Because each boy is going to like someone different, something that appeals to him, especially.

Here's something else to keep in mind: Not one boy — not one — reported that his "dream girl" turned into a "dream come true." In reality, it didn't work out that way. After the boy got to really know the dream girl, then a) he found he didn't like her, b) it fizzled out, c) they became friends but nothing more. So much for the girl of his dreams. It was more fun dreaming. When it comes to liking a girl, boys end up liking something entirely different than what they imagined!

Excuse Me, Wanna Dance?

Until not so long ago, it was the boy's responsibility to make the first approach. He would see some girl he felt attracted to, take a chance, maybe stumble and bumble, and possibly get rejected. Girls waited and waited and waited for a boy.

But everything has changed for girls and boys. Girls can now make that first approach if they want to. They don't have to sit or stand and wait to be chosen. Girls have different ways of approaching boys (as you will see if you read what girls have to say about boys!).

Boys, though, will always follow the age-old tradition. While they often feel flattered when girls do the approaching and generally like it, they still do the asking whether at a disco dance, during the school day, on the beach, or anywhere there are boys and girls together.

Sammy, 14, will go right up to a girl and take the plunge:

> "I'll say, 'What's your name?' I'll ask where she lives. Or if she's around a lot. Or what kind of sports she likes. It depends where I see her."

Sammy admitted he was often rejected. Quite possibly because some girls don't care for the F.B.I. treatment.

Sometimes boys collect more rejections than they care to honestly admit, even to themselves, but they keep going. Would you like to know how they feel? This might help you to understand why that cute boy in the corner stands and stares but never walks over to you.

Jeremy, 14, admits very truthfully:

> "Once or twice I've gone up to a girl, but not really very many times. If I'm at a dance or something, I ask them to dance and while we're dancing or after, I just talk. It's not that easy to just go up to someone."

Perhaps you've spotted a Richie, 13, who stands around listening to what the girl has to say first before he makes his move:

> "I listen to find out how she talks to other people. After that I usually go up and act crazy and do stuff like that. I make a lot of jokes or say wild things. Girls love it. It always works."

Does it? Or does he just think so? Many girls might not appreciate Richie moving in like a five-piece band. But what they might not suspect is that all his yuk-yukking and noise are a cover-up. Richie is actually a little shy. A girl might think he's funny, but "unreal." She might not realize the truth. Many boys are shy at this age. They differ only in their disguises and cover-ups.

Keith, 14, can talk about it:

> "I'm sort of shy and it's hard for me to approach a girl. I would never walk up and say something like, 'Hey, babe . . .' You know, that kind of approach. I look instead for conversation. Something I think she would enjoy talking about."

Conversation Is the Key

The next time you're at a dance or a party or near the locker of someone you think is very, very cute and nice, remember this: *No matter what boys say or do, most of them are somewhat shy!*

If you wait for him to make that first approach you're missing meeting a lot of nice boys Don't wait. Don't hesitate. Make your own approach. It all depends on *how* you go about doing it.

Here's how a typically shy boy, Danny, 13, makes his approach:

> "I guess I go up and say 'hello.' Then I ask her what her name is. This depends now. If it was at school, I'd say, 'hello . . . what's your name . . . where do you live?' That's it. Then I'd talk to the person day after day. To get to know her better. Then maybe I'd ask her out."

You could do something like that, if that's your style. But ask *him* out? There's the kicker. But why not? If you get to know a person, slowly, as a friend, like Danny does, you could ask him over to do homework, to an upcoming dance, or you could have a little party and invite him to get to know him even better. You can use different approaches. Sometimes you don't have to work so hard because the boy will pick up on it and will ask you out.

An opportunity to talk to a boy you think you like may come up on the spur of the moment. You might be standing at the same bus stop or working side by side on a school activity. Say *anything*, to get a conversation rolling.

Robbie, 13, tells girls what *not* to do:

> "There was a girl and she spotted me and came up to me. I liked it a lot. But then she kept following me and sent me all those notes. It's just too outgoing. I didn't care for it. But if a girl just walked up to me at a party and asked me if I wanted to dance, I'd probably say 'yes.' It depends on the girl."

A boy looks to see if the girl is smiling and if she might be someone who is fun and nice to know. He doesn't need an invitation to be tortured.

If you ask a boy to dance at a party, you might get rejected for your efforts but you can applaud yourself for trying. (You might find you don't even like the boy after you've talked to him!) Pestering a boy to death with notes and calls,

11

when he'd rather be left alone, is pointless. It's the best way to lose the boy, forever.

It's more fun (and much more sensible) to become the girl you want to be, inside and out, rather than daydream about the girl you think boys will like. Besides, the Real You is the girl real boys will really like.

GETTING TO KNOW YOU

If it's already been established that most boys are shy around girls (until they get to know you), then you know it's hard to get to know them. Even casually. Until the time when a boy's cover-up chips away and the real boy decides it's safe to come out of hiding, it can be maddening. Because *you* have to make conversation with *him,* or try. And sometimes they don't help much.

Some girls think boys do this on purpose because they have bad manners, are just plain dumb, or . . . don't like them. Meanwhile the girl does all the work. Sometimes you might even feel you are making a fool out of yourself as you talk and talk, trying desperately to make conversation while he seems so cool and collected and slightly detached. Most of the time he is neither cool nor collected. But detached does fit. The boy is suffering from a strange, nervous disorder which can descend suddenly, without warning. It's called "clamming up."

Clamming Up

Girls clam up, too, though sometimes in a different way. Boys say clamming up is like being invaded by an alien being from another planet. This being doesn't know what to say or do and is temporarily frozen in space. So boys will sit or stand and wear a silly smile, unable to say much of anything. Their palms feel sweaty and sticky, their throats feel parched. No thoughts run through their minds to come out of their mouths. They are not themselves.

Maybe you never knew boys went through all this. Maybe you thought they were only "cool." Here's how some boys described what actually happens to them when they're with a girl:

Alan, 13, often feels funny or shy around girls he would like to meet:

> "A lot of times I will clam up. I'm not the kind of person that will just go up to a girl and say, "Hey, you want to go out?" It takes me a while. I do clam up and I hate it. But I'm not a cold person."

Joey, 14, has a common symptom:

> "I start stuttering. That happens a lot. I have a crush on a girl right now. I want to say the perfect thing, so I never can say anything. Then I try to stay away because I don't have anything thought up. Even today I was thinking if I try not to consider her as someone I like and would like to go out with, but just as another person, someone I'm not attracted to, I might do better. It would be easier to talk to her. I'm going to try that."

Ward, 14, says:

> "I just got out of a boys' boarding school. It's hard for me to relate to a lot of the girls

in my school now because I don't really know how to start a conversation and take out girls and stuff like that. I don't know basically a lot about how it's done."

There it is. Before you give up or get disgusted with a boy you are trying to talk to, you have to understand this one basic fact: Boys have feelings much like girls do.

Have you ever heard of the term body language? That's when words (or in the case of boys — lack of words) may tell you something, but facial expressions, eyes, or body movement may be a dead giveaway. It's useful for you to be able to read a boy's body language so you can decide if he's shy or just someone you don't want to get to know better.

It's not all that difficult. Just look for these signs:

His eyes: Are they bright, smiling, and gazing into yours or are they down on the floor or bouncing to the walls and windows? If he can't look you in the eye or can't look at you at all, he's feeling nervous. But if he's looking around the room at a dance or party, watch out. He may merely be scanning the room for a girl, or other girls, while talking to you. That's just plain rude.

His face: Is his forehead all crinkled up? Do all the lines on his face, especially around his mouth, droop downward? Maybe his smile looks like it was plastered on. Those are all signs of a face that's worried and not relaxed. He feels uncomfortable. If he doesn't make you feel too uncomfortable, you might want to wait a little longer and give him a chance.

His body: There is one way to see if his body language is giving away shyness. Watch how he dances. If he dances easily, but when the music stops he moves awkwardly, he feels somewhat shy. He loses himself in the music and movement, but actually he's unsure of himself when he's not dancing.

Boys were asked if there was anything girls could do to make matters better for them when they find themselves clamming up. Many times it becomes impossible for them to help themselves.

Wiley, 14, has this hint:

> "Girls could keep the conversation going. When I clam up, I retreat back into my circle of friends. A friend comes along and I just latch on to him and walk away from the girl. I guess I give up."

Too easily, many girls would say. And heaven knows, girls do try to start conversations . . . and keep them going! But now you know why boys might walk away. Not because you did anything wrong or looked funny, but simply because they were incapable of doing anything right and felt funny!

Jesse, 12, complains about feeling shy around girls:

> "Lots of times girls laugh and give you funny looks. They do this when their girlfriends

are around. I don't feel as embarrassed talking to them alone as when their friends are around. It's hard to talk to a girl when she's surrounded by a bunch of her friends."

Admit it. Isn't one way of protecting yourself from sudden attacks of shyness to move with a group of bodyguards, otherwise known as your girlfriends? That can throw a boy. It's just one more bit of knowledge if you want to understand boys better.

Mark, 13, confessed, depressingly, when asked if there was anything girls could do:

"I don't think there's too much they can do about it, really."

Making It Easier

But girls can make it easier for boys they wish to get to know better. Girls are more verbal. At your age, words do come easier to girls. Even boys you think are just so "cool" and couldn't possibly clam up do just that, sometimes, around girls.

Mickey, 16, is one of the school leaders, yet he does admit to clamming up:

"When I'm not going steady with a girl, I feel shy around girls. I really do. But now that I'm going steady with someone, I don't feel funny at all talking to the other girls."

Here are some ideas to keep in mind when you're talking to a boy that will make it easier for both of you:

17

1. Ask him questions. If you want to get a boy talking, the easiest way is to ask him questions. Questions about himself, his schoolwork, or anything you can think of that you both are interested in.

2. Resort to small talk. You know what small talk is, don't you? It's when your mother passes Mrs. Smith on the street and says, "Morning, Mrs. Smith, nice weather we've been having, isn't it?" And Mrs. Smith says, "Oh, yes, much nicer than last year. Last year it was cold around this time of the year." And, to your amazement, they actually continue this nonsense conversation until one or the other smiles and says, "It's been nice chatting with you. Bye now!" What has really happened? Well, your mother and Mrs. Smith don't know each other very well but they want to exchange some pleasantries and so they talk about the weather. Small talk can be useful to you, too. You don't have to talk about the weather, but you could small-talk the food in the school cafeteria, the last game, or something that has been on page one in all the newspapers. Small talk is merely a way of loosening up. It could lead to bigger talk later.

3. Smile. You can put someone at ease with a simple thing like a smile. But sometimes you think you're smiling and you're really not. That's because you're nervous, too. Really remember to smile at him every once in a while. A phony grin that seems to hang suspended in space and looks like you're auditioning for a toothpaste commer-

18

cial won't do it for you. Be sincere and let your smile say, "I'm friendly" and "I like you."

4. Listen. This is an art. People can tell when you're listening. It shows on your face. You don't look away or appear to be tuning out or falling asleep. You don't have your mind on something else. You're not rehearsing what to say when he stops talking (and not hearing what he has to say) so you can say something clever when he finishes. Listen to what he is saying and look at him while he's saying it. If you really listen well you'll have a much better idea of who the boy is and whether you want to spend any time with him.

5. Give honest compliments. Everybody in this world can find something nice to say about someone else to their face. "I like your sweater." "I thought the way you answered that question in class was fantastic!" "You have the greatest sense of humor . . ." Sound terribly phony? It's really not. Think back to all the times you did intend to give a compliment, it was on tip of your tongue, but it just didn't come out. When you're with a boy, an insincere compliment won't do. But if you have anything you genuinely admire about him and want to say something, do it. The purpose of a compliment, in this situation, is not to make you look good but to help the boy relax and feel more at ease.

It's also important to know when to give up. One almost has to give up on a boy that's hopelessly shy. Knowing when to give up is a feeling that you experience after you've tried and tried and, after a certain point, it just doesn't matter all that much anymore. To keep on trying after that point would be ridiculous.

Honesty Is the Best Policy

In the beginning of a relationship, there is a word that's very important. The word is . . . HONESTY. Many years ago girls grew up with the understanding that their role was to flirt and play games and act helpless. They never told the truth about how they were feeling or what they thought. Even today some adults will throw up their hands and shake their heads muttering, "These kids today. Everything has to be so honest." That attitude might seem mysterious to you. That's because it belongs to another generation. Boys and girls of today are much more honest.

If you are not honest, if you play games, you will do things like make your little sister answer the phone when he calls so he will think you're out with someone else and get jealous. You will also be setting a pattern that will lead to a lifetime of dishonest, confusing relationships with boys and men. It's a bad and destructive habit.

Howie, 14, talks about how he felt when a girl was dishonest with him:

> "I wanted to ask this girl out. We were friendly. So I did, but she refused to give me an answer. She just kept me waiting and waiting. Every time I brought up the sub-

ject, she would put me off. Finally, I asked for an answer. So she said, 'I don't think so.' I thought that was pretty unfair. She could have told me that in the beginning. I'm not even friends with her anymore."

If you are honest and open with the boy you like, from the beginning, you'll never regret it. Perhaps you feel you have to study and can't meet him after school. Tell him why. If he doesn't like that, instead of doing what he wants you to, ask yourself if this is the best boyfriend for you. You don't have to lie or make up excuses to do what you want. There's no reason to lie to yourself, either, by giving in all the time.

Honesty also applies to anger. If you feel angry, let him know. You don't have to stage a temper tantrum, just tell him the reason. The same is true for sadness and joy. Figure out what you feel and share it with him.

Liking someone can be great fun. Crying into your homework over someone you can't communicate with is a miserable experience and a damaging waste of your time. If you can honestly relate, early on, with the boy you like, you'll not only have a boyfriend but also a good friend.

DATING

There's a certain style to dating. It varies from age to age and crowd to crowd. It also has to do with where you live.

Girls can ask boys out, as mentioned before. They can ask them over to do homework or to an outside dance. They can ask them to play tennis, go bicycling or jogging, or to share in any activity which is a common interest. They can even ask a boy to dinner if they think it would be fun and their parents wouldn't mind. Anything a girl feels comfortable with is fine.

If a boy doesn't want to go, he's free to say "no thanks," just as you are when a boy asks you out. If you want to ask a boy somewhere, ask yourself if the fear of his "no" might be holding you back. Then tell yourself it's not the worst thing in the world. At least you know, once and for all, he's not interested at the moment.

Boys were asked if they would mind if a girl asked them out. Some typical answers went something like this:

Philip, 13:

"It sounds okay to me."

Sandy, 15:

"No, I wouldn't mind. Not at all."

Casimir, 14:

> "I guess it would take some of the pressure off boys always having to do the asking."

Another style is the one of choice. If you don't want to date, don't feel pressured by what the others do. Your style is not to date yet, but to wait. That's okay. Many girls feel exactly the way you do.

To date or wait is a personal decision. The way boys feel about dating is also personal and their styles differ, too.

Boys Talk About Dating

Barry, 14, talks about what makes him feel comfortable:

> "Well, at first, on a date, I get nervous. After a while it goes away. In a group you're sort of competing with your friends, so on a date it's easier."

John, 16, has a relaxed style of dating:

> "I live in a suburban area. Most of the time we don't go out and spend money. Sometimes we just hang out with friends. There's a footbridge in our town and we hang around there. We do a little partying. Or I'll go over to a girl's house and watch some TV or something. We either go with the group or sometimes we'll go out alone. It varies."

Robert, 13, dates only on the weekends:

"We go out to a movie or she comes over to my house. Or I'll go over to her house."

Don, 14, has a favorite date who is also his best friend:

"I have one friend, Melissa. We usually get together on Fridays. I'll go over to her house and watch TV or something. We like those old movies because we're both very interested in acting. She's part of a steady group that I always go with. That's how we date. Very casually."

All this is quite a far cry from the old-fashioned dating system that is something of a ritual. Undoubtedly you'll discover this for yourself as you date and get older. You can choose to take part or not. The old-fashioned dating system is still alive and flourishing even now, even among boys and girls your age. Tom, 16, gives a revealing example of just how this works.

The Case of the Old-Fashioned Date

(taken word for word from a talk with Tom)

Q: When you go out with your girlfriend, do you go on formal dates?

A: Yes.

Q: Does she pay her own way? Many boys and girls prefer to go dutch.

A: No, she does not go dutch.

Q: Do you prefer it that way?

A: Well, let's put it this way. I've never really thought about it. I've just naturally insisted. My dad pays for everything, no matter who he is taking out. It's probably something I got from him. I always pay for everything. Do I prefer it that way? Well sometimes when I look at my supply of cash on hand, I'm a little bit short from paying all the time. But it's something I do.

Q: Do you think it's the boy's responsibility to pay for everything?

A: You might say I'm the old-fashioned type. The way I was brought up, you take a girl out and you pay. Of course there are exceptions to the rule. We just had our rival football game and we both had a bet on who would win. She lost and she owes me a dinner, but even though she owes me a dinner and is supposed to pay, I'll work it out so I pick up the check.

Q: Do you think she wants to treat you?

A: Oh, yes. She probably does.

Q: Is she happy with this style of dating?

A: Well, my little brother happened to hear her talking to somebody once and she said, "Tom treats me like a princess." This is a quote from her own mouth. She likes it. And I like to think she likes it.

Tom's way is one way of dating. Your mother might have done it, your grandmother most certainly did it this way, and maybe your older sisters are dating this way now. It's not wrong. It's not right. It's a way that is considered proper and correct by many women and girls. It might appeal to you. Maybe you're thinking, "Wow! His lucky girlfriend. Look, he treats her like a princess." Then again, you may think, "Yuchh, she can't even treat him to a dinner if she wants to. He probably tells her what to do."

Most boys and girls are more flexible in their dating habits. And that includes a girl paying her own way. Here's what other boys say about who pays.

Billy, 14, is loose:

> "Sometimes I go dutch and sometimes I don't. It depends on the person and where you're going."

Marty, 15, isn't exactly rigid, either:

> "Oh, you know, it works different ways all the time. Some nights I like to pay her way. Sometimes we pay together. Some nights she feels like treating me. It depends on how much money the other person has, I guess."

Here's a case where the girlfriend isn't too un-bending about what she has been taught is correct and proper. Eric, 16, says:

> "Actually, she's always been told the boy is supposed to pay and she feels that way. But she really doesn't mind paying because just the other night we went to the movies and she paid for her ticket. She knew I didn't have any money and we couldn't go unless she did. I think it works out much better that way, but I don't think it *has* to be dutch. Maybe one time we'll go out and I'll pay for the whole thing. Maybe another time,

if she gets some money and we want to go somewhere, she'll treat."

Usually boys and girls of the same crowd get approximately the same allowances. Unless the boy has a part-time job, it isn't *always* fair for the boy to pay for everything, always, all the time. Actually it means you're going out with his father or whoever gives him his spending money. If you go out just to have fun and do something together, it really doesn't matter who pays.

What does matter is that you speak up if you think something is unfair about who's paying for the date. If you keep feelings and thoughts inside, especially about money, you're going to feel hostile and end up ruining your date.

GOING STEADY

Many books for girls will give you the same advice about going steady: "Don't do it. You're too young. Go out with a lot of boys and have fun." This is sensible advice but it may not work for you. As Roger, 13, says, "Dating one girl one week and then asking another girl out for something the next week is terribly old-fashioned. Most kids go steady."

But don't misunderstand. If you don't feel like going steady, there's nothing wrong with you. Many girls refuse to limit themselves to one boy at a time. Many girls don't even care about dating right now. But if you do care about going steady, there is a right way and a wrong way to go about it.

Going steady to most girls follows this imaginary script: You walk out of school . . . he's waiting to walk you home . . . you do your homework together. In the evening you meet your crowd. Together. On the weekends you're together. You have someone that is special. You feel fantastic all the time.

Going steady can be like that, though most boys and girls aren't always glued to each other quite that much. Going with someone can be a good experience and a happy time. But you need one basic ingredient. The boy. Sometimes boys make going steady an impossible achievement. They're not always willing partners.

Some boys thrive on going steady. They love it. But others loathe it. If a boy you like doesn't want to go steady, or does it badly, there's often a reason. It may not seem there is to you, or it may seem like a silly reason, but it does help to understand how some boys feel.

Boys Speak Out on Going Steady

In answer to the simple, harmless question, "Have you ever gone steady?" Jay, 14, got angry:

> "At first it was fun. But now it's the reason I don't want to go out with any of the girls in my grade. I have to see them every single day and if we had a fight the night before, we'd have to make up in school because we see each other all the time. Toward the end of my relationship, it was a mess. A real mess. The girl I'm going with now goes to another school. It works much better for me. I'll never do what I did before, that's for sure."

Conclusion: Jay had a messy and painful experience. He thinks he's learned a lesson: Don't get too involved with a girl in school; she's too close for comfort. He has decided to stay away from the enemy, or all the girls he's with on a day-to-day basis. Any girl who is interested in Jay and doesn't want to transfer to another school has a slim chance. Many boys who feel the same way Jay does won't say as much, but won't date girls from their school, either.

Chad, 14, tells about a typical dilemma that keeps more boys from going steady:

> "My friends didn't want me to go out with her. They were my same age. They would follow us wherever we went. They were really serious about it and we never had a moment's peace. Even when we went to her basement to do homework you could see these eyes peering through the little windows near the ceiling. I guess they made it their mission in life to break us up. Anyway, they succeeded. I just couldn't take the pressure anymore. I didn't want to lose the friendship of my best friends."

Analysis: Probably at 16, Chad will be less likely to swap his girlfriend for the company of his boy friends. Chad is a sweet person who tried to be all things to all people. He crumbled, finally, in the face of peer pressure. Peer pressure is the feeling that you have to conform to what your friends do or say. If you don't conform, you lose them. Peer pressure is sometimes what makes people go steady in the first place.

Later, Chad admitted: "Well, everyone was going steady. I wanted to see what it was like. I didn't want to feel left out."

That's the *wrong* reason to go steady. Then along came his boy friends (who obviously were not going steady) and this determined collection of crazies fought hard not to lose their pal to the enemy: a girl. A case of arrested development, a girl might think. Ugh, revolting — they act like they're 10! But remember, sometimes boys grow up more slowly than girls and Chad wasn't ready to go steady. Unfortunately, some of the boys you might like to settle down with for a semester or two or more are going to be just like Chad. They'd rather spend most of the time with their buddies. They're not ready, no matter how hard you may fight, for a steady girlfriend.

Kenny, 13, is also strongly against going steady. After his experience, it's easy to see why:

> "Here's what happened. I found out she liked me and I thought she was cute so I asked her out. Also, all my friends kept saying, 'Ask her out, go ahead.' So I did and I liked her. But she kept bothering me. At lunch I'd be sitting with my friends and she'd be sitting with her girlfriends. She'd get so angry because I wouldn't go over and say hello or eat with her instead. I mean, she really got mad. She said I didn't talk to her enough in school. She told me to my face. She said, 'You don't spend enough time with me.' I think it's stupid to be confined to one person. I never had any fun. I felt like I wasn't allowed to talk to anyone else."

Comment: Kenny picked the wrong girl to go steady with. He chose Miss Appearances. She wants him to come up to her in the lunchroom and during school because it gives her status with

31

her friends. They know she has a boyfriend. Had she been a little less demanding and not acted so possessively, she might have kept him. But for what? Kenny is obviously not ready yet to cut it as part of a couple. Maybe he did ignore this girl too much by her standards. Perhaps he felt, "Help! She's telling me what to do. What is she, my mother? Get me out of this!" Many boys are like Kenny. They have had bad experiences with other girls. They may like you and like girls in general but refuse to go steady.

If there's one lesson to memorize, it's just this: *Don't break your heart on boys who don't want to go steady.*

Going steady is not for everyone. Just because everyone seems to be doing it doesn't mean you should plunge right in. Think it over first. Think of some of the advantages and disadvantages — such as those listed below. Then add anything else you can think of to fit your own particular circumstances.

Advantages:

You have someone all the time. You "belong."

You're in love and it's lovely.

You always know where you're going and who you're going with.

You're part of a couple and you do things with other couples.

You have someone to be affectionate with.

You're not lonely.

He can be your best friend.

Disadvantages:

If you so much look at another boy, you'll blow the whole relationship.

Recovering from those draining fights takes all your energy.

Seeing the same boy day after day sometimes gets a little boring.

Seeing the same coupled friends day after day sometimes gets a little boring.

Only the girls waiting for you to break up care that you go steady.

He begins to go a little further with sex than you want to.

You feel lonely. Even when he's around.

You can't always call him a friend. Only a boyfriend.

Scott, 15, says going steady has its advantages and disadvantages for a boy:

> "I always feel better about myself when a girl likes me and I like her and we go together. Still, I know it traps you when you see the same girl all the time. But, the advantage for me is that I know I have someone."

Going steady for most boys and girls has advantages and disadvantages. Like anything in life, it's time to think seriously about ending it when the disadvantages outweigh the advantages.

How To Go Steady Happily

Unfortunately, some girls often play roles they think might be appropriate when they are attached to a boy. They pretend they are married or act out the idea of what they think the woman's role should be. It's usually a passive role and one that very few women who are married play.

A lot of boys commented on this attitude that they have noticed in some girls.

Andrew, 13, has this complaint:

> "Well, if you're not going to get married, you shouldn't go steady. I had a girlfriend who acted like we were married. I couldn't do anything. She was always around. It just got silly after a while."

Here are some suggestions you can keep in mind when you go steady that will avoid this:

1. **Be your own person.** You may be part of a couple, but you're also a complete individual. Very few people in this modern age of mobility marry their junior-high-school sweethearts. To each relationship there's a beginning, middle, and end. If you lose yourself somewhere in the middle by becoming so much a part of him, you won't know who *you* are when it ends.

2. **Take part in the planning.** Does he always plan the places you go? Does he pick the latest science fiction movie, a game instead of a private picnic, staying in instead of going out? If you've never suggested something to do and really re-

sent his making plans all the time or had your suggestion overruled, you've started a bad pattern. Start over now. If there are things *you* want to do, say so.

3. Call him. If you're going steady, it doesn't make sense for you to sit around and wait for that magical *brrinnng*! . . . it's·HIM! Or after you come skidding out of the shower on a bar of soap the heart-sinking "Sorry, it's not for you." If you're going with someone and feel funny calling, just realize that many girls feel funny calling, but that doesn't stop them from doing it.

4. Get angry. Don't be afraid to get angry. It's okay to do with your boyfriend. If you feel angry, say something! If you continuously swallow your anger or are afraid to show it, it will go somewhere else. Some girls get physically sick, others become depressed, and still others go around kicking the cat or taking out their bottled-up anger on people who can't defend themselves.

When you're angry you can explode to your girlfriends, but anger directed at the wrong person still remains bottled-up anger. Tell *him*. You don't have to shout or scream or pout. Just zero in on whatever it is that is bothering you. The best time to do this is right at the moment it happens. Expressing your anger, when you have it, will help your relationship. When two people are close they sometimes do get angry with each other. Saying something about anger is part of being truthful. When there's never any anger in a relationship it tends to be flat, false, and, before you know it, finished.

5. Have other friends. The importance of having other friends, male as well as female, can't be stressed enough. Shutting all the friendship doors for a boy is bound to backfire one day. When the never-never land you've created with him disappears, you will feel very lonely indeed. Keep your friends. If you're stereotyped as a couple in your group, keep up acquaintanceships and friendships in other groups. If you break up, you may find you have to change groups. It's not an impossibility. Others have done it. But it's easier if you keep the friendship channels always open.

BREAKING UP

It was spring and he asked you to go steady. Every morning you woke up to sunshine flooding through your window and couldn't wait to start the day. Every afternoon you walked home from school holding hands with him. Spring drifted into summer and you wished it would never end. You saw him every day. Then autumn came, school started, and the leaves changed colors and began to fall off the trees. You saw him less and less because he said he was busy. Then it was winter and cold, dark, and dreary. One day he told you it was over. You're walking home from school alone now. Just yesterday you saw him holding hands with someone else.

Soap opera? No, a true story. When the boy you have been going steady with decides it's over, it can be a long, lonely time, and yes, it hurts. You might think, "How could anyone I thought so highly of be capable of hurting me so much?"

Mark, 16, is the boy who broke up with the girl in the story above:

"We went out in the spring and summer. I was the one to break it off eventually. I did it in person. I just said, 'No, I don't think this will work anymore.' Bye-bye and all that. I hate to say this because it sounds chauvinistic, but she was shocked. She really liked me a whole lot and, as it turned out, I didn't think quite as much of her as she did of me.

Unraveling Mark: He sounds cruel, doesn't he? But he was honest with his girlfriend and he did tell her in person. Many boys just stop calling or ignore the girl because they are afraid she'll create a scene when they break up with her. Maybe Mark's girlfriend felt as if her world had crumbled beneath her, but at least nothing was left to doubt.

Dennis, 14, had trouble ending it but finally succeeded:

> "We broke up twice, in a way. The first time she and I agreed not to go out anymore. Then she called me and said she still wanted to. We went out once or twice more and finally I told her I just didn't want to go out with her anymore. Whatever feeling I had for her, which there definitely used to be, had just gone away. I decided there was no point in it anymore and I broke it off."

Figuring out Dennis: Dennis knew the relationship had passed its prime, but his girlfriend still wanted to hang on to it. He tried for a while, but found the relationship was dead, stale. He did the honest thing for both of them when he ended it. It's better, of course, when the breaking up is mutual. Whenever one decides it's definitely finished, the other is bound to have regrets. But a relationship with a boy can't usually be brought to life once it's over. There's nothing there.

Think of friends you once had that you never get together with anymore. Could you revive that warm feeling of friendship you once shared? Most likely you have nothing in common anymore with those old friends. It's the same between a boy and a girl. They grow in different directions and the relationship changes. It doesn't happen overnight, though the realization might. It's best to break up. People who are growing don't go back again to where they were.

Chad, 14, who told about breaking up with his girlfriend (in the previous chapter) because of peer pressure from his boy friends, admits:

> "Yes, it was my decision to break up. I couldn't take it anymore. I wanted to do it before Christmas vacation and I just couldn't say anything because I felt so funny. I couldn't talk. She got it out of me and ended up saying all the stuff I wanted to say."

Analyzing Chad: Before, we concluded that Chad was too immature to handle going steady. His boy friends won and his girlfriend lost. But did she? Judging from what he says, the truth is that in the end she did the breaking up for the tongue-tied Chad. Any girl can do what she did. At some time she reviewed the relationship and found it lacking. You can periodically review your relationship. Ask yourself what is really happening. Are you happy or hanging on? If something is wrong, talk it over. This is what Chad's girlfriend did. If she had not read her situation correctly, knew they were in trouble, no one would have talked about it. She would have ended up spending her Christmas holidays with a clammed-up Chad and his buddies trailing them like the secret service.

Your Rejection and How To Handle It

How often have you laughed and called someone or something a "reject"? Well, welcome to the club if a boy breaks up with you. But there's a distinct difference. You have been rejected but YOU are *not* a reject. You might think so for the first tragic couple of hours or days. But always remember this piece of logic: You are only rejected as a steady. You are not a reject as a person. You may not feel especially terrific when it happens, but in time you'll honestly feel you're a terrific person again.

The First Thing To Do: Let yourself feel bad. If the news strikes suddenly, unexpectedly in school, slip into the restroom and have a little cry if you feel like it. But don't leave school until the final bell. After school, act any way you like (short of setting fire to his house). Cry some more if you like, cry on a girlfriend's shoulder, take a long walk, play ball, or put on some records and dance. This will help release all those understandably painful feelings and start getting the hurt out of your system.

Take a tip from Jeff, 14, who found himself in the same boat one day:

> "She told me she just didn't want to go out with me anymore. I still wanted to go out with her, but I guess she didn't, so . . . I started running and just kept running until I got tired."

It's destructive to make things worse by refusing to do your homework, being nasty to your family (especially if they don't know what's bothering you), or doing something to hurt yourself. But go ahead and feel sorry for yourself. Just make sure you do it for *only one night*. After that it's time to start picking up the pieces and putting yourself back together again.

GETTING THROUGH IT: The next morning you are not going to feel as happy and joyful as you will in the future. For a second when you first wake up you might, but then you'll remember and you'll feel sad and heavy. Just getting through this period of time is rough. You'll see him in school. Perhaps with another girl (ouch!). It will take the greatest effort to talk to your friends and keep your mind on what the teacher is saying. Everything will look as if a master painter took a paint brush and colored everything a dreary gray.

Boys have to just get through it too. George, 14, confesses:

> "When she wanted to end it, I was really broken up about it. Whenever she was

around, my nerves got jangled. It was really hard for me, but after a while I was able to talk to her just as a friend."

Getting through it means just that. Do your best. Think of yourself as a broken bone. It takes time to heal. TIME is the key word. Everything gets better in time. For some it will take just a short time, for others longer. Think back on your life to something bad that happened. Does it seem so tragic now? Time has a way of healing broken bones and broken hearts.

Mike, 12, got over it finally with that old faithful remedy — TIME:

"It took day after day until after a while I stopped feeling bad. Then one day I realized I didn't like her anymore. But it was gradual, you know?"

Here is a guideline to follow while you're passing time:

1. **Don't keep everything inside.** Talk to your girlfriends or friends who are boys. Friends can be very sympathetic and understanding. But don't make that all you ever talk about or they will get tired of you.

2. **Go out.** Don't stay home wandering what he is doing and who he is doing it with. Go out with friends. Being with people will take your mind off your problem.

3. **Don't look back.** It won't help you one bit to think over all the good times you had with him. You can't bring back the past, no matter how much you may wish to or how well you can

remember every detail. Each second that ticks by on the clock makes the past second history. The past exists only in your mind. Let go of it and live in the present. You'll have a great future if you do.

4. **Have patience.** It's a great disappointment. One you think you'll never get over. There's nothing to do but experience it and wait, with patience, for the unhappiness to disappear. Know it will. You just might find that it wasn't such a bad experience after all — because you got through it and grew up a little.

5. **Don't settle for just anybody.** The temptation when you've been hurt is to jump into another relationship, any relationship, fast. That could make matters even worse. You might make a mistake and get hurt all over again. Make sure you're ready for someone else and actually like that person before you go steady again.

THE LAST PHASE: It almost seems to happen overnight. Suddenly you're happy again. You can really laugh. It's not surprising and it's not an overnight miracle. You have healed.

When you're feeling like your new self again, and dating and having fun, don't be surprised if your old boyfriend looks as if he's attracted. He is. It's not your imagination. But it's not exactly a healthy attraction.

Remember Dennis, 14, who, earlier in this chapter, decided there was no point in continuing a stale relationship and broke up with a girlfriend who tried to hang on? You may be surprised at the outcome.

He says innocently:

> "It was sort of strange when I saw her hanging around with other boys in school. I felt bad. You know, I went out with her and all of a sudden, it's . . . no more."

All of a sudden it's no more! He broke up with her! Now *he* feels badly because he sees her with other boys. What's going on here?

First, let's hear from Brad, 14, who has a similar story to tell:

> "I broke up with her. We told each other we would remain friends, but it didn't work out that way. When she started liking other boys, I really got jealous."

Let's call this the Old Boyfriend Syndrome. It can be maddening. Here's what happens. They decide they don't want you, but they don't want you to have anyone else. All it is, really, is that green-eyed monster, jealousy, rearing its head.

When You Break Up with Him

Though you may swear it looks otherwise, the fact is boys have the same feelings as girls. They get hurt. They feel rejected. They just may not always show it. Have you ever told a boy you were through? He may not have said much, no emotion may have flickered across his face, but he felt something. Especially if he wasn't expecting it. Here is how some boys felt when their steady girlfriends broke up with them.

Jimmy, 15, felt very hurt and a little bitter:

"When I first met her — I'm pretty shy, you know, but she was too — she was friends with my cousin. At first I couldn't think of anything to say. But then we really got along well. I liked her. Then one day I found out she was going out with someone else. My friend told me. I said, 'What?!' So I asked her and she told me she didn't want to go steady anymore. I was hurt but I wouldn't let her see it. If she wanted to go out with me again I'd say, 'no way!' "

Frank, 13, never had a reason to break up with his girlfriend. But she broke up with him:

"She's really nice looking. Just about one of the best-looking girls in our school. I thought she might break up with me but I wasn't sure. Then one day her best friend called me up and said, 'Frankie, Julie doesn't want to go out with you anymore.' Just like that, you know? I felt like a jerk. I was mad."

Both of these girlfriends are examples of How Not To Break Up with a Boy. Frank would have preferred it if his girlfriend had called him herself and not gotten a girlfriend to deliver the news for her. Jimmy would much rather have had his girlfriend tell him they were through before a friend told him she had started going out with another boy. Both of these girls probably never intended to be cruel. But they were both afraid to face their boyfriends.

They were afraid to tell the boys they wanted to break up because they were not assertive. They were not able to confront their boyfriends with the simple truth. So they caused unnecessary pain and confusion on top of the hurt the boys already felt. Saying you're through to a boy might be hard to do, but it's something that should be done.

The best way to break up comes from a boy. Take this advice from Jack, 16, who goes to a boy/girl boarding school:

> "In my school everyone breaks up the same way. You just say you want to talk to the person. When you're alone you tell the person that it's not working out or whatever you think is wrong with the relationship. Do it simply and quickly. It's much better to be frank."

Jack and his friends do it this way for a very good reason. Picture a small school in the country where everyone knows one another very well. Everyone eats dinner together and in the evening they watch TV and do their homework together. No one goes home at night! They have to make a clean, honest break. There are less than 50 boys and girls in the whole school. They have to get along with each other! So they have to be considerate.

At Jack's school, couples pair up and break off quite frequently. They hardly consider breaking up with someone the end of their world. And neither should you.

FRIENDS WHO ARE BOYS

Many years ago, girls were brought up to think only of a boy as "the opposite sex." That's because the differences between the two sexes were stressed. Now everything is changed. Boys *are* different, of course, but you are alike enough to be good friends. As for the differences—well, that's what makes boy/girl friendships so very special.

Having a boy for a friend gives you a viewpoint you'll never get from a close girlfriend. It also teaches you a lot about boys and how they think. If you already have friends who are boys, or boyFRIENDS, you know how great it can be. But if your school or crowd is divided into boy and girl groups as separate as enemy camps (or if you would like to have more boyFRIENDS), you might like to know how or if this can work.

Boys Talk About GirlFRIENDS

Eddie, 14, talks about his good friend, Lisa:

> "Lisa's my best friend. I'm friends with most of the girls in my group because I don't really want to go out with them. But I'm not close friends like I am with Lisa. She can tell me what a girl feels about things. In most cases it's much easier to talk to her than a friend who's a boy."

What can you learn from Eddie and Lisa? Eddie can be friends with most of the girls in his group. Well, that's not surprising. He doesn't want to go out with any of them. It's Lisa, though, who is his special friend, his best friend. He can learn from her what girls are like because she's obviously open and honest and warm. No wonder she's his best friend if he can honestly talk to her. With the boys Eddie might feel he has to prove himself or live up to what he thinks they expect of him. It would be impossible to show his real feelings. Whereas with Lisa, he can relax and be himself.

Ethan, 16, goes to a school where there are many boy/girl friendships:

> "I'm good friends with most all of the girls in the upper classes. Our school is small, so everyone knows everyone else. You're friends with everybody, boy or girl. I've gotten to know some girls really well and when it comes to friendships — it doesn't matter to me whether they're boys or girls."

Ethan doesn't draw his friendship line squarely in the middle of the sexes. As Ethan grows older, he'll have an edge when it comes to relating to women. He knows how to be friends with them. When you meet an "Ethan" type, see if you can tell the difference between his relaxed friendliness and boys who treat you as a "date" or as a "girl."

It's almost hard to believe when you watch the boys you know horsing around with each other, but a boy in a boy/girl friendship can be extremely gentle and kind and will give of himself a great deal.

Paul, 13, gave his girlFRIEND this advice when she came to him with a problem:

> "There's this one girl I talk to a lot. We're good friends. She calls me if she ever has a problem. One time she had a boyfriend and there was another boy who liked her and kept asking her out. She wasn't sure what to do. I sort of gave her advice. I told her it was really her decision. But if she really liked the guy she was going out with, she should sit down and talk to him about it and explain to him exactly what was happening. Then she could decide whom she liked best. She did talk to her boyfriend and she decided to keep going out with him."

It's fairly obvious that the advice Paul gave his girlFRIEND is the way he would like to be treated by a girl in the same situation. This was helpful to his girlFRIEND who needed to talk to a boy about this sticky problem.

It should go without saying, however, that if your boyFRIEND gives you advice you consider bad for you — don't take it!

Boys value the friendships of girls for the same reason. They may not always ask for advice, but they are eager to learn what girls are like.

Greg, 12, admits gratefully:

"If I'm saying or doing something that will make the girls who are my friends angry, then I know I'm acting wrong. It helps me with the girls I date too."

Because in the real sense of the words you *are* opposite sexes, complications can arise to interfere with the friendship. Love, for example.

It happened to Blake, 15:

"We started out as good friends. She used to tell me all her problems. I would help her out. Now I find myself really liking her. Only trouble is she's going with my best friend. She knows how much I like her and there is a possibility they might break up, but I would never do anything to break them up. They're my best friends. Funny, I never expected this to happen."

It's a happy accident when you and your good friend feel it's "something more." It's not something you can plan on or even dream will happen, but it has a way of sneaking up on two good friends. The trouble here is it snuck up on one good friend.

One rule to memorize is simply this: *Find a boyFRIEND that's just a friend. Not a boyfriend.*

Easy to say but hard to do, you may be sighing. How can you find a boyFRIEND when the boys in your grade are one step removed from planting spiders on the girls' chairs and the older boys already have girlFRIENDS. The girls in their grade.

If you can genuinely say that most of the boys you know are decidedly subhuman creatures, it is not going to be easy to find a boyFRIEND. Try opening up a little and start looking at boys differently. It just may be that there *are* boys available, but you have been boxed in by that old attitude. You relate to people as only girls to girls, boys to boys, or girls to boyfriends. That's limiting.

Boys feel the same way, sometimes. Walter, 15, would like to have girlFRIENDS, but he doesn't find it that easy:

> "I do have girlfriends to say hello to or to talk to about school with, but I don't call them on the phone or tell them my problems or anything like that. I'd like to, but there's no one I can do that with."

To find these special boy friendships other girls treasure, here are some pointers:

1. Spot the "different boy" in your crowd or school. Maybe he isn't macho or good looking. Maybe he's sweet and sensitive, perhaps a little shy and quiet. Just maybe there's great friendship potential there, but no romantic possibilities. And maybe you overlooked him because that is the way you judged him before.

2. Go outside of school to make new friends. Having a good friend who goes to another school is not so unusual. Many girls find boy-

FRIENDS this way. You might look for this new friend in your church or synagogue, in an after-school activity away from school, or right in your own neighborhood. He might go to a different type of school.

3. Turn an old relationship into a new friend-ship. Norm, 13, reported that after he broke up with his girlfriend he waited a while and they became very good friends. He says, "I found it easier to talk to her when she wasn't my girl-friend." A lot of people find this to be true. Some-times social pressures and anxieties prevent a boy and girl from being completely relaxed. Once they drop the idea of romance, they take off the masks and become real friends. Some girls find they never really knew the boy they were going with until they broke up and became just friends.

4. Be open and friendly to boys. That's how friendships develop normally. You talk and joke and become friends. But if you cancel out boys as being a different species, you'll never get close enough to make friends with them. If you're friendly, that friendship with a boy might just blossom on its own.

It's delightfully easy to be friends with a boy. Just think of him as a good friend first and as a boy, second. Make sure you have no romantic feelings for him, nor he for you. If this arises, talk it over with him. If you're honest and up front you'll be good friends. That's what real friend-ship is all about, anyway.

Here's the story of a good friendship between a boy and a girl. Sean, 14, tells it:

> "Elise is my good friend. We're in the same grade. One day she came over after school and really got to know my brother, who's a grade higher. They started to like each other and went steady. Until summer. He broke up with her and left to become a camp counselor. She really felt bad. We spent the whole summer together just talking and doing things. At the end of the summer she met someone she really likes. I'm happy for her."

It's nice to have a boy who's a friend. If you want a boyFRIEND, really want one, you'll find one. Good friendships are never forgotten. Don't be surprised if, years from now, you remember more about a boyFRIEND than the boyfriend who broke your heart in the ninth grade.

BOY TALK

The boys interviewed were all asked this question: "What *really* bothers you about girls?" They didn't hesitate to answer. You'll find their answers revealing, sometimes surprising, maybe even a little amusing. It all depends on you.

If what they have to say produces a twinge of red-hot anger, try to see it from a boy's point of view. Besides, maybe anger is a good reaction. It gets you to thinking, and when you think you sometimes change. That's how you grow. Remember no one's perfect. They aren't, certainly. But neither are you. There's always room to improve.

Here are some typical boys talking about some typical girls they know.

Joel, 13, talks about the effect clothes have on the girls he knows:

> "They like stupid things. They're more apt to have peer pressure. Take pants. One girl in my class has 20 pairs of a certain kind of jeans. Another has 10 pairs. The competition between the girls is unbelievable. I have three pairs of pants for school and the rest of my clothes are for dress. Girls are so materialistic. If I found a girl who wasn't like all the rest, I would really like her. And if I found her, that would be amazing."

Looking nice and dressing in clothes that make you look good are important to a girl. What Joel is complaining about is the competition for clothes among girls, which is a special kind of peer pressure. There's something to be learned here, because boys do notice it. It's very hard to go on a date with your clothes closet. Boys don't judge you by your clothes; they judge you for yourself.

Helpful hint: Putting too much attention into clothes is just a crutch. Clothes are just a cover-up to give you confidence. The Real You is actually shy. Try depending on your clothes less and depending on yourself more. You'll be thinking less about your girlfriends' approval and more about being a likeable person.

Charles, 13, talks about a girl who had no qualms when it came to calling a boy. That was her problem:

> "I never had a chance to call this girl. As soon as I got home from school she called. Then she would call back before dinner and a few times later. Sometimes I would be out with my friend in the driveway playing basketball. My mother would yell for me to come in — I had a phone call. She called a lot. When she broke up with me, I felt bad. But that was one of the reasons I got over her so easily — no more phone calls."

Certainly Charles's girlfriend couldn't have had that much to say. She was possessive and used the telephone to say it. She was actually insecure.

It wasn't that Charles minded that she called, but that she never stopped calling. She was exercising a control over his time.

Helpful hint: Don't go overboard with a boy. There's nothing wrong in calling him, though. A good measure of how many times to call him would be approximately how many he calls you. Sometimes girls, even girls who are normally shy, will suddenly become obsessed with a boy, making him their whole life. Girls don't like boys who make pests of themselves and neither do boys. Don't go phone crazy.

Jamie, 13, complains about having to take sides:

> "Girls can get you very embarrassed. I have a girlfriend and she started screaming at my best boy friend because she was mad at him. I didn't know what to do. I ended up taking the side of my girlfriend and having a fight with my boy friend. Why did she have to drag me into her fight? She feels I have to be on her side all the time because we go together."

What happened to Jamie is a small incident that is connected to a larger problem. That problem is called ownership. The belief that going together means you own each other. It means you must be alike and agree on everything, even if you disagree. If one of his friends gets angry with you, he'll just have to be angry with that friend too, even if he doesn't even know what caused the fight.

Helpful hint: Boys do not appreciate being owned. They might be good-natured about it as Jamie has tried to be, but one day there's going to be an explosion. Sooner or later people who realize they are being owned will rebel. They are likely to leave. Do *you* honestly want to be owned? Sometimes it's not easy to see that it is happening. But if you let your boyfriend have his own opinions and feelings about people and let him make his own choices and decisions, you won't own him. Insist that he let you do the same and he won't own you.

Kent, 14, can't stand a certain behavior trait he's noticed in many girls:

> "What bothers me most about girls? Oh boy, this is easy. It's the girls who go around acting stuck-up. You know — unfriendly. They always have a nasty little remark for everything. I can't stand that. I'm not talking about the way they act toward me, but toward everything in general. It's an attitude. You can just tell that type of girl. The girl I go out with is not like that at all. She's very friendly."

Actually, those girls Kent despises aren't really stuck-up. They are very unsure of themselves. It's a case of one-half shyness and one-half peer pressure. The stuck-up girls have developed a cover-up that hides their feelings of insecurity and works for them. Every member of the stuck-up group clings together and must conform to this nose-in-the-air attitude. Pooh-poohing this and snickering at that has become a safe habit. They would never admit, not even to themselves, that deep, deep down they don't see themselves as superior to everyone else at all. They really feel inferior.

Helpful hint: If you can honestly admit you've been acting stuck-up with your girlfriends, ask yourself if you could act that way if you were by yourself. What if your whole crowd of friends were to transfer to another school? You would be very lonely. Far from being stuck-up, you'd have to try your best to be friendly. If you didn't want to be all alone. Why not pretend your friends have already left and try being more friendly right now?

Larry, 14, has a problem that seems similar:

> "There are some girls in my grade that I don't like because they think they're so much above everyone else. They go running after senior boys. That really gets to me. When girls go around acting better than anyone else, I don't like it."

In case you haven't guessed, the girls in Larry's grade are not wholly at fault. They simply like older boys. Again, in adolescence, or the ages from about 12 to 18, girls do mature and develop faster than boys in certain areas. They can't always find something in common with the boys in their class. It's helpful to know, though, that some of the boys your age may feel exactly the same way Larry does. You can then understand why they are so hard to get along with.

Helpful hint: Be nice to the boys in your class no matter how immature they seem. Besides, you can never tell when one of them might magically mature and interest you.

Now that boys have gotten what they have to say about girls off their chests, let's find out what is in their hearts. The same exact group of boys also spoke of their feelings toward love. They would *never* tell a girl all this to her face.

Boys Talk About Love

Joel, 13:

> "I know that later on I'll feel different, but it's like when you're around a certain girl and you feel really happy. You're glad to be with that girl."

Charles, 13:

> "Love is when you care about somebody very much and they care about you too."

Jamie, 13:

> "It's a feeling toward someone that would be different from anything I've ever experienced. I can't put a name to it. But I think I'll know it when I see it."

Kent, 14:

> "It's very hard to talk to my father about this. He said, 'You're just infatuated.' I don't necessarily agree with him. I love my best

59

friend who is a girl and I love my other friends and my parents. But this kind of love is different."

Larry, 14:

"Love is when you really want to be with a girl and you want to be everything to her but not quite everything. You want to be yourself, too. You feel very comfortable. You feel very strongly for her and you would really do a lot for her. Love's a really hard question to answer. It's something you just feel so strongly about."

Love will change and grow as you change and grow. Love is a little of everything the boys said. It's caring for somebody very much, feeling comfortable with that person, and being happy just to spend time with him or her. It's also hard to define in words.

Maury, 14, explains why he thinks it can't be defined:

"There are so many different kinds of love. I love my friends. I love different people. But with a girl, it's those feelings and a whole new set of feelings on top. You can't define love for everybody because everybody has different feelings."

Older people might chalk up your feelings to mere infatuation, a word that means, to them, that you are in love with the idea of love. They think of love as leading to a permanent relationship. There are different levels of love you will feel as you mature. Yours, now, may be very real to you.

Now find out what *girls* have to say about *boys*.

Girls Talk About Boys

MR. COOL

There she is. The prettiest girl in your school. One day you get up enough nerve to stride up to her and say, "How would you like to go out Friday night?" She looks up at you, smiling sweetly under her long, oh so long, lowered eyelashes and says, "I can't. I already have a date. Thanks anyway, Ralphie." And she walks away.

Ralphie? Your name is Fred. You must have blown it.

So you wander home, wallowing in self-pity, and fantasize about being the type of boy she *would* go out with. Let's see now. He would have to be tall, athletic, macho, and very, very cool.

This is a common mistake boys make. They compare themselves to the big hero, the mythical Mr. Cool they think all girls look for. True, some girls prefer that type. They might want to be Miss Cool. But, in reality, they are anything from shy to dependent to superficial to spoiled. You may be suprised to find out what most girls like in a boy.

Not every girl wants the athletic type, trembles to the sound of a macho command, or turns to putty over someone *you* think they would have to like — a Mr. Cool. Most girls don't like that at all.

Jennifer, 14, wastes no time telling what attracts her to a boy:

> "Okay. I like clean. I don't like a lot of acne or greasy hair or oily skin. I like really bright eyes and a smile. That's basically it."

Jennifer probably sounds like your mom checking to see if your fingernails are clean. But the odd truth about girls is simply this: Boys who appear clean are attractive to them. Better clean than cool.

Lydia, 12, knows exactly what she likes about a boy she sees for the first time:

> "I look at his eyes. And I look at his mouth to see if he's smiling. The smile tells me if he likes me."

Question: What happened to cool and macho? Ninety-nine out of a hundred girls would gladly have warm and friendly instead.

That's not to say looks don't matter when it comes to attracting a girl. They do. All of your dating life, girls will judge you somewhat by your appearance. You will do the same with them. Looks do matter, but what you think of as good looking will not always be what a girl thinks of as good looking.

To make this a little easier to understand, here are two examples of girls who swore their first attraction was looks. But as they kept talking, it was obvious they didn't stop at movie-star, muscle-bound looks.

Joyce, 14, is drawn to a certain kind of look:

"I like a good-looking boy, but not the stereotyped cute look. Just someone who seems interesting and a nice person. Generally, I can tell right away if they are open or drawn back."

Tammy, 14, looks for someone who's a little more than good looking:

"I look for a boy that looks good physically and who is handsome. Someone who seems to be having fun outdoors. If I see some boy doing something I'd like to do, like playing tennis or ball or running, I would know that's a person who shares my interests."

Pamela, 15, couldn't be more clear or brief:

"I like a guy who looks cute. Who doesn't look like a bum."

But don't get the impression that girls are shopping for deodorized boys who always gargle with mouthwash. Girls want *real* boys and they want to get to know the boy inside as soon as possible.

Kathy, 13, knows the type of boy she's attracted to and why:

"I'm sort of old-fashioned. I like the guy to be polite, intelligent, and have lots of personality."

Marla, 14, does like a certain kind of "cool." The kind more accurately called confident:

> "I am attracted to a boy by the way he handles himself. The way he smiles. If he's at ease and can make conversation easily. The things he says to other people. And what he's wearing."

Daydreaming about being the kind of boy all girls will automatically fall for is a waste of time. Different types of girls like different kinds of boys. It's best to take what you have, work on bringing out your best qualities, and just be yourself. The catch here, of course, is the phrase *best qualities*. Do you *know* what yours are?

Do you have a good sense of humor? If so, don't be afraid to show it. Are you shy and quiet? You can turn that into a quality girls will like. Not every girl wants to be with a boy who is loud and noisy and constantly hogging center stage. All you have to do is learn to talk more, remember to smile, and listen to what girls are saying. Are you good at artwork, play the harmonica by ear, or have a knack for cooking? Those interests used to be considered feminine, but not anymore. If you have a talent that's part of you, don't hide it. Many girls will be interested in sharing your interest.

Here's a simple guide guaranteed to help you feel more confident. If you pay attention to these details, obvious though they may seem, girls will pay attention to you. It's that simple.

Lookin' Good Guide to Getting Girls

1. **Clean up your skin.** Clean up your skin and you'll clean up your act. That means washing your face twice a day with soap and water. It means eating the right foods (not all junk food) and remembering to eat fresh, green vegetables, Use an astringent on your face if it's very oily. If you have an advanced case of acne you can't handle yourself, go to a dermatologist, or skin doctor.

2. **Pay attention to your clothes.** This doesn't mean you have to show up dressed like Boy Model or Disco Danny. It merely means that your clothes are clean, fit well, and serve the purpose of making you look good and feel good. Pamela, 14, confesses that she always checks to see what a boy is wearing. "I am clothes-conscious and I hate to see a boy with baggy pants or a sweater that looks dirty."

3. **Do something about BO.** Yes, body odor. It can get you every time. Especially in history after gym when you were too busy fooling around to jump into the shower. It also won't get you the girl you like. If she's had her nose up in the air when you've come near her, maybe that's why. The remedy is simple. Shower every day and especially after gym and after school sports practices.

4. **Take care of your hair.** An otherwise good-looking boy can hide forever under a head of hair that is neglected. It's easy to have good-looking hair. All you need is healthy hair. To

have that, shampoo it as often as you need to. Once a week for very dry hair and much more than once a week for oily hair. When you get your hair cut, choose a barber that will give you a cut that looks right on you and not like it was designed for someone else. If you have dandruff, use a special dandruff shampoo. The difference between hair that shines with good health and hair that droops from lack of care is the difference that may change your looks.

5. Don't forget to smile. You'd be surprised how many people do. Your mind might be on a test, a party that's coming up, or a slight from someone that happened five minutes ago. You march down the hall or street looking as if you'll growl if anyone even approaches you. That includes a girl you may be interested in. This is not to say, either, that you must go around all day grinning idiotically when you don't feel like smiling. It's just a reminder. Don't forget you have a face and if it's frowning, no one will know you are not unhappy with them. No one can read your mind. Remember to smile when you see people you know. It will tell them you are friendly and approachable.

Margaret, 15, talks about the importance of a smile:

"The first time I saw him I said, 'I really would like to know him.' He wasn't that good looking or anything. I just noticed something about him. I guess it was the way he smiled at me."

This guide is simple, easy to follow and re-member, and important for a reason other than looking and feeling your best. You already know the type of boys girls are attracted to at first sight. What you may not know, though, is that girls, once attracted, will approach you. You won't always know they are doing this because girls can have subtle ways of approaching boys they find attractive.

Camille, 14, describes what happens when she has a "mad crush" on someone she hasn't been introduced to yet:

> "He'll be standing there and I'll see him. If it's somewhere other than school, I might go up and say, 'Hey, don't I know you from somewhere?' If it's at school I might say, 'Don't your parents know my parents?' or, 'You're in my study hall, aren't you?' Anything I can think of."

What Camille is trying to do is start a conver-sation. All you will remember is that you talked to her. It won't be that obvious that she came up especially because she thought you were at-tractive. Girls often make their approaches some-thing like this. Unlike boys, they would feel un-comfortable doing anything more direct.

Debby, 15, puts herself in a strategic position:

> "If it was in the schoolroom, I'd go up to someone who was standing near him and start talking to that person, just to be close to him. Then I'd turn and make a comment

to him or something like that. There's this boy I used to like whose locker is across the hall from my friends' lockers. So I would go all the way upstairs and talk to my friends. He would be standing right near, watching us. Then he'd be in the conversation. I did this on purpose and he did pick up on it. He asked me out."

Don't get the idea that *every* girl who brushes against your shoulder in the hall, or asks you what time it is or if you roller skate, is madly in love with you. Do keep your eye open for the girl who is trying, in her own way, to make the approach. If you like her as well, it will be easy to help her along.

One of the reasons girls want to make their approach to a boy almost unnoticeable is because they are afraid of a rejection. Not that boys like it, but eventually they get used to those little rejections and learn to take them in their stride. With girls it's different. They feel that if they disguise their approach, no one will know what they are up to. If they come right out and ask you for a date (though some girls will!), it will be a big tragedy if you said "no thanks."

Girls are also very concerned about appearing popular because they think boys will like them better. Rachael, 12, goes to great lengths when she goes to a dance:

"First I ask the really shy boys to dance. They usually never ask and never do the asking. Then the other boys ask me to dance

72

when they see I'm dancing or in the middle of things."

You might find you are attracted to a girl like Rachael, who seems popular and sparkling. But don't overlook the girl standing near the potted plant, nibbling on a pretzel. She may not have the social skills of the other girls, but she may be nicer than all of them put together.

And forget about Mr. Cool. Girls are looking for Mr. Nice. That's easy to be. Just be yourself and don't feel you have to put on an act. The majority of girls in this world are more interested in a boy they think is nice than a boy they can't even communicate with.

RELATING

Have you ever noticed that in class many girls speak clearly and answer questions without mumbling? In the halls they talk with their friends. They never seem to be at a loss for words. Like you are when you're with them.

Many other girls talk, talk, talk until a boy comes up. Then they stare silently into space. They do the same thing a lot of boys complain about. They clam up. Suddenly they are panic-striken, suddenly they have *nothing* to say, and suddenly they want to turn and run.

Donna, 14, has a problem talking easily sometimes:

> "If I'm trying to impress a boy, then I usually end up becoming very shy. I don't know what to say. Or I end up making a fool of myself. I talk to him but not much."

Maria, 15, doesn't like to put on an "act":

> "I think I know about one or two boys, plus my little brother, that I can really talk to easily. I find it very difficult. If you try to be flirtatious, you're putting up a barrier between yourself and the boy. I've never been very good at that, anyway."

Kathy, 14, finds it hard to talk to a boy easily and casually:

> "I get really nervous. Really tense. I try and come up with things to say, because if there's ever a pause between conversations, I just don't know what to do. If it gets really bad, I make some excuse and just leave."

Kathy brings up an interesting point. When there's a pause or a silence in conversation, people do tend to squirm and feel awkward. But those silences in conversations are sometimes natural. It's just when you don't know somone that they seem to stretch out for hours and hours.

Here's a good tip: Next time you notice talking has stopped when you are with a girl you've just met, try to say something that will start the conversation going again.

There's something to be learned from Joanne, 15:

> "If it's a one-to-one conversation with a boy, I always find myself leading the conversation. I usually ask questions, since boys will answer them. Sometimes I find it very hard to get a boy to contribute to the conversation."

Ask any question to end that pause. Ask her if her ears are pierced or if she likes basketball or if she plays a musical instrument. The question is not important. The fact that you start up the conversation with a new topic is.

Joanne brings up something else, something almost every girl interviewed seemed concerned about. Boys do nothing to help girls have a conversation with them. While you might be floundering for words but acting as if you couldn't care less, they're racking their brains for something, anything, to say.

Fern, 14, complains:

> "The only subject the boys in my class will talk about is homework. Then I think to myself — what would I be talking about to a girl? On Monday I'll say 'Hi, how was your weekend? What did you do?' Usually the boys will say, 'nothing.'"

Here are some suggestions that will help, until you get to know her better, so talking will come naturally.

1. Compliment her. Never give a phony compliment. It can be something as harmless as "You know, you have great eyes," or "That's a nice sweater," or "I love your laugh." It may seem ridiculous, but it will make her more at ease and the conversation will flow easier.

2. Ask questions. As Joanne revealed, that's a girl's technique. Why not make it yours? You don't have to wait for a break in the conversation to ask questions. Ask them any time. Ask about her and about anything else. She will think you are the best conversationalist in the world because you're pulling your share of the conversation load.

3. Find a common interest. Perhaps you've found yourself in conversations like this: "Oh, you went to the same grade school? No kidding! I went there until we moved up here." Then you discuss all the teachers and mutual friends you might have as if grade school meant everything in the world to you. Or — "Your cousin is Gary Smittergitten? I know him! He goes to my Sunday School." Then Gary gets discussed as if he were running for President. But you may not always be so lucky as to discover a mutual friend or place or activity. In that case, you have got to talk until you find something to use to relax and open the conversation up a little more freely. A common interest. It could be music, a hobby, a sport, even a favorite food.

4. Talk about anything. The worst mistake you can make with a girl you would like to get to know better is to let her do all the talking and take responsibility for the whole conversation. If you're clammed up, don't feel you have to be a witty conversationalist — just say anything. Talking about how much it rained, how Christmas is so commercial, or about a movie you saw isn't brilliant, but it will do. Any conversation has a very good chance of leading to a real conversation, and after that, there's nothing to worry about.

5. When all else fails. If all else fails, you can always do what Sarah, 15, does. She says, "When I feel shy, I just say, 'I feel shy.' I know I leave myself open when I do that because he knows and I can't put on an act. But it works for me in the long run." Has Sarah ever gotten a sarcastic reply or rude remark? Nope, never. Have boys responded to her comment and tried to make her feel more at ease? Yes, always.

Could a boy say something like that? Why not? If you do it right. You could say to a girl you don't know very well, "You know, I'm not a brilliant conversationalist when I first meet a girl because I'm just a little shy. Until I get to know the person." Or something like that. Chances are the girl will say, or think, "Oh, I know just how you feel." Besides, if all else fails, what have you got to lose!

Girls Give Advice to Boys

Cynthia, 14, advises:

> "Relax. Be more comfortable. Boys are so tense sometimes. Also, if you approach them, they automatically think you have a crush on them or something silly like that."

If a girl approaches you, think of her as friendly and nothing more. If that's all it is, you just may have a new friend. If it's something more, your macho attitude won't drive her away.

Deidre, 13, would say to boys, if she could:

> "'Hey, you could make this a lot easier on me if you would talk openly. Or just talk! So I don't feel nervous.' When I like a boy and he's shy and I'm shy that makes me even shyer."

It's very possible that you could lose yourself so deeply in your own foggy cloud of shyness that you will fail to realize something very important. She might be just as shy. When shy is confronted with shy, the result is zilch.

Here is what Susan, 15, (who is a little shy sometimes) does when she meets a very shy boy:

> "I would give up on a guy who won't talk. A guy you can't get to say anything. I can't take it if he's not willing to at least try to talk."

Relating, talking, smiling, being with a girl and doing fun things together were not created to give you hours of misery. Just remember that being with a girl you like and know is not at all the same as struggling to make conversation when you are first meeting her.

The way to get to know a girl better and go out and get along with her better is by following this one important one-word rule: *Talk!*

And keep on talking to her. If you let her carry the whole conversation, she'll walk away from you sooner or later. You just might find, after getting to know a girl very well, that she's also a friend.

GOING OUT

Going out, or dating, means different things to different boys, depending on the customs of your crowd. What kinds of dates do girls prefer? It varies. Here's a sampling of just how much:

Maxine, 14:

> "I basically like hanging out in a group. We all went out on dates right away in sixth and seventh grade. Now we are sort of exhausted with each other."

Danielle, 12:

> "We usually go to the doughnut shop after school. That's a date."

Tina, 14:

> "We don't date. No. It's mostly group things or doing something after school."

Marcy, 13:

> "We do date. We might go to a concert or a movie. Or we just might walk around or something like that."

You might be going out already, or you might feel so uncomfortable just thinking about it you've decided you can wait. That's okay, too. Some boys need more time.

If it's not the easiest thing in the world to go out with a girl, keep in mind, also, that you are changing and growing. That's not easy, either. Your body is growing, your ideas are changing, and it seems everywhere around you the people you love are acting differently, too. Can this be? Or is it your imagination? It's very likely your family and friends are responding to the new changes in you.

For example, your father: Suddenly he's telling you *how* to go out. He's even giving you some extra money. Doesn't he know all you're going to do is go over to Mary Beth's house, hang around, and then take a walk? It's probably hard for your dad to understand the newer, more casual way of dating. In his day he had to follow rigid rules or didn't get to take the girl out. You could explain to him what it's like now. It could be possible, also, that he might feel a little jealous of "you kids" and your free style. Back in his day he had to work hard to date.

Your mother: This is sometimes hard to understand, but it happens to every boy and sometimes even to grown men. Your mother will suddenly realize that you are not her little boy anymore. You're going out with girls. She might be jealous of the girls you bring around. Either your mom will act overly interested or ignore them completely. Maybe your growing up reminds her that she's growing older. You might try being extra-specially nice to your mother until she gets used to the idea.

Your friends: Some of them will turn out to be a real pain in the neck. These are the ones who want everything to stay just as it was. All boys and no girls. But everything can't be as it was because boys grow up. That is what's happening to you. Some of your friends might be a little behind you but, don't worry, one day they'll catch up. Right now it might be a touchy subject. You'll spend some time with your buddies and some time with your girlfriend. You could try to discuss your feelings with your friends, if you think it will help. There's no reason to choose sides. If it comes to that, just make sure you do what *you* really want to do and not what other people want you to do.

Girls Talk About Going Out

Toby, 13, has a problem which may seem familiar:

> "I feel a little intimidated by my friends because a lot of them don't date and haven't gotten involved with guys. Whenever I feel that someone likes me or I like somebody I won't make a big effort for this person because then I would be the only one going out. I'm really afraid of people calling me names. If my other girlfriends went out, I would feel easier about it. Or I would want a boyfriend more."

Figuring out Toby: It's not so hard to figure her out when you figure that boys do the same thing. You may think you are getting rejected but she's afraid to date because her girlfriends don't yet. If this is true of a girl you like, why not throw a party? Invite her girlfriends. Hopefully a few of them will begin to date, too.

Jeannie, 14, has a peculiar problem that could confuse a boy:

> "Usually I'll start liking a guy. The more distant he seems, the more I'll like him. But as soon as he starts noticing me and liking me, I lose interest. I feel this most when a guy likes me first. I might think he's nice but as soon as I hear that he really likes me, I just don't like him anymore."

Figuring out Jeannie: It's not easy, because Jeannie can't figure herself out. You may very well run into a lot of "Jeannies" in your dating life. Oh, terrific, you're probably thinking. You start to like her and she stops liking you. Jeannie is afraid of getting involved with a boy. She loves the meeting and the excitement of getting to know a boy, but as soon as she suspects he might be a boyfriend, she runs away. She stops liking him. This is a stage many girls of her age are in now. Most likely she'll just outgrow it. Unfortunately, though, some girls grow into women and still feel this way. What's a boy to do? Nothing. The more you pursue a girl like this, the worse you're going to make it. Go on to the next girl and forget about the "Jeannies." If she changes next year, try again.

A Story Within a Story

Here's a little story. It's about a boy called Stuart, 14, and a girl he liked very much. Her name is Vicki and she's 14, too. To get more out of this story, pretend you're Stuart and ask yourself, every time he has a decision to make, what you would have done if you were him.

It all started when he broke up with his girlfriend, Lynn. She asked him if he would like to be friends though they weren't going out together anymore. This came as a surprise and after a few days he finally agreed. Though he wasn't sure at first, he decided he had never had a good friend who was a girl and he wanted to try. They became best friends. Lynn started dating another boy but Stuart was without a girlfriend.

Lynn asked Stuart if he wanted to meet her friend, Vicki, who went to another school. Lynn told him they were perfect for each other. She was sure they would get along. (Not surprising, friends of friends usually do all like each other.) She told Stuart and he thought about it and said "no." He was fixed up once before and it was a disaster.

But the damage was done. Lynn was so sure that Stuart would want to go out with Vicki she had already told her about him. Vicki thought Stuart sounded nice and really wanted to meet him. Reluctantly, Stuart called Vicki. Not once but several times. To his surprise they seemed to talk about everything and anything for hours and hours. He wasn't so sure, though, if he should ask her out. Maybe he would think she was unattractive or silly. Lynn suggested that they just all have lunch together somewhere. Stuart agreed.

What Stuart didn't know was how very excited Vicki was. She loved the sound of his voice and thought he was smart and nice. The night before they all met, she stayed on the phone for an hour with Lynn planning what she should wear.

Lunch was easy and casual, and afterward, Stuart took the bus home with Vicki. At his stop he said to her, "Well, have a good weekend." He liked her a lot but he didn't want her to know. He didn't think she liked him.

But Vicki thought he was one of the nicest boys she had ever met. Lynn had been right. She waited for him to call. She was sure he would call right away but he didn't. He was afraid of a rejection. Of course she could have called him, but she didn't want to call him first. Calling *him* first wasn't her style. Not a boy like that. Soon she was wondering if he liked her at all.

It's easy to see what has happened here. They both liked each other but they were afraid to show it. Stuart acted cool and Vicki followed his lead in the sense that she couldn't give the impression that she liked him and would like to go out with him. The story of Vicki and Stuart might have been a continuation of other "cool" games except that their good friend, Lynn, straightened everything out. She was able to assure Vicki that Stuart would probably call soon. She also assured Stuart that Vicki liked him and he should call. They are going together today.

You might not have a third person to keep score for you. Many boys and girls act in much the same way that Stuart and Vicki did. Why play guessing games? When you're out with a girl you can let her know that you like her or think she's nice. You don't have to go overboard.

What Girls Say About Who Pays

Dorey, 14, is for it:

> "I just don't think it's fair that he should have to pay for all of it. We both get the same allowance."

Carolyn, 15, is violently against paying her own way but is passionately for women's rights:

> "I prefer the boy to pay. I believe that women should have equal rights but I don't like it when boys don't open doors for me and things like that. Not all of them know this about me. One boy asked me out and suggested we split the check. I hinted around and asked if someone told him I was for Women's Lib. He said he had heard and I kept talking about it, too. He finally said, 'Well, I'll treat you this time.' I guess he thought women should be equal all the way down the line."

Analysis: What do you think of Carolyn? What would you have done in the same situation? The truth is that if Carolyn was sincerely, 100 percent for women's rights, she probably would have insisted on paying for her share. Apparently she loves to talk about it but doesn't fully live it. On the other hand, would the boy have asked her to split the check if he didn't think that's what Women's Liberation was all about? In that respect, Carolyn had a right to feel hurt and angry. She probably sensed he thought he could get away without paying for her or was testing her. But, when you invite a girl somewhere, you *should* pay. You can agree on who pays for what after you decide if you're going to keep on seeing each other. Who *really* seems more liberated — Carolyn, who talks and talks, or Dorey, who does what she feels is fair?

What's important about going out is not who pays but that both you and your date agree on what is fair. If either of you feels something is unfair, talk about it. It's what is left unsaid and makes you angry that can cause problems. Going out can be fun only if you make it so. That's easy. Just enjoy yourself and make sure the girl enjoys herself, too.

GOING TOGETHER

Girls have a lot of special magazines and books telling them exactly what to do and how to act. Boys are a little left out. When it comes to going steadily with a girl, you're left to make your own mistakes.

Often you won't know what to do or say. Why did she get angry and hang up on you? Why did she suddenly turn on her deep-freeze act when just yesterday she was so friendly?

There's a certain cycle in "going together" that hardly ever varies. The cycle follows this pattern:

1. You meet a girl you like and you go out. It's wonderful.

2. You start going together. It happens mutually or one of you brings up the subject and you both agree on a formal declaration of going-togetherism.

3. Everything is just fine. Going together is great.

4. Something's wrong. You can sense it (or, unfortunately, sometimes you can't). But you can't quite put your finger on what's wrong.

5. Yesterday you broke up.

Courtney, 15, says, mystified:

"I don't know what happened. It was so fabulous and we had so much fun. Then it seemed to just fizzle out. It turned out to be a number-one disappointment."

Sound familiar? Actually, up until Number 4, you really have no problem. This happy state can last two hours, five days, eight weeks, six months, or longer. Number 4 is the turning point. It can drag on and on or result in a girl telling you it's over five minutes after you begin to suspect something might be wrong. Or worse, you may never suspect anything until it's all over and you try to figure out what happened.

Sometimes you just can't understand what went wrong. When exactly did it stop working? That's the catchy part. You may only have thought your relationship was working, but it wasn't. It wasn't open and it wasn't honest. When you and your girlfriend can't talk about troubling incidents that are bound to come up, feelings stay bottled up inside. This can happen again and again, anger can build, and before you know it, you're both on an imaginary sled racing downhill. Where you are going to crash? Later you ask, "Hey, what happened?"

Girls Tell What Went Wrong

Barbara, 14, couldn't find the words to tell her boyfriend what was actually happening:

"It was really fun. It was great. Until I started growing up and he started growing down. He just never changed and he was really immature. I had the same phone conversation with him for a year. I wasn't going out with anyone else at the time. It was awful."

That's old Number 4, alright. But in this case, there was no stopping it from happening. Barbara never lied to herself; she just didn't know what to say to her boyfriend. Her big mistake, if she felt "it was awful," was to keep the relationship creaking along for a year. Sometimes it's hard to understand, but boys and girls are constantly growing and changing. You might think she's suddenly acting silly or phony, and you would probably be right. But she has changed and so will your relationship. You may find you don't have that much to say to each other except when you fight. When you sense a relationship is dragging you down, don't wait for it to do more damage. Part immediately and you'll part friends before you become bitter enemies.

Robin, 14, tried to be something she wasn't until one day everything went wrong:

"I've gone with someone steadily and I felt kind of confined. I like flirting. I really don't like going steady right now. My boyfriend took it all very seriously and I just didn't. I didn't like having just one boyfriend. One day I finally told him. It's not right for me now. Maybe when I'm 16 I'll think it's better."

Robin was honest. She tried to go steady and it just didn't work for her. But her boyfriend who "took it all very seriously" was probably trying to figure out what went wrong. He couldn't have chosen more unwisely. It can hurt very deeply when you like a girl and you see her flirting with other boys. If and when that happens, why not suggest that you *not* go steady. Leave it open. You can see each other but be free to see other people. Also, without pressure, she just may decide on her own she's ready to go steady.

Samantha, 15, wasn't able to see what was around the corner:

> "I went with someone this past summer and it was a very good experience. It was wonderful, in fact. Until something happened that disappointed me. I got tremendously close with this guy. We were like best friends. Then sex came into the picture. More than I was ready for. The only way he seemed to want to continue the relationship was to go further than just kissing. I didn't really want to. I really wasn't ready for anything like that. So that was it."

This can present a problem to a girl like Samantha. Put yourself in Samantha's shoes. You've got a boyfriend. You're happy. He's your best friend. One night he's not your best friend anymore. You don't know if there was a full moon or what. But suddenly he's a combination octopus, wrestler, and vacuum cleaner all rolled into one. You feel frightened and surprised. But most of all, disappointed. He's interested in a lot more than just kissing. And not only that, if you're not — the two of you are through! (You can step out of Samantha's shoes now.) Can you understand how the girl feels? Samantha wouldn't go along with her boyfriend. Some girls will, though. But if they put up a fight first, you might be right to suspect that part of them doesn't want to and the other part is more afraid of losing a boyfriend.

Life can become very complicated when you toss in a three-letter word like sex and you're still in your teens. It's the smart boy and girl who knows that more than just bodies are involved. You have emotions, fears, feelings, and doubts that are not nearly as mature as your body. That's where the complications come in.

Summer Romance

This is a special category of going together that can happen to any boy, or girl, when they go away for the summer to stay with relatives, travel with their families, or go to camp.

Francine, 14, tells what happened to her:

> "My family took a summer cottage on the lake. I met this boy the day we got there. He became my best friend but I liked him a lot, too. If we were older, we would have gotten married, probably. When I had to go home and he came over to say good-bye, it was really sad. He lives so far away we can't even call each other. But I'm hoping to save my baby-sitting money so I can go and visit him. That's really all I do is babysit. There's no one I'm interested in here."

The biggest mistake Francine or anyone can make is to decide not to plunge into the new school year and make friends. It's a big mistake because it won't help things. Summer romances are special partly because they take place at a certain time of your life in a different place. Sometimes that's what makes them seem so wonderful. But ask yourself this: If that girl went to your school and you went steady, would it be exactly the same? Do you think you would feel exactly the same way about her as you did when you were both far away?

You might agree with Penny, 14, who says:

> "We went together over the summer. We don't live anywhere near each other. It had to end. It was just something that happened over the summer. It wouldn't work out."

The Right and Wrong Way To Go with a Girl

Right: You have one special girl. She's always there for you. She's your friend.

Wrong: She's not there for you because you're never honest with each other. You may like each other, but you're not really friends.

Right: It makes you feel good just to be with her or talk to her.

Wrong: It makes you feel good because you know you're running the show. You're giving all the orders, you're calling all the shots, and she will do anything you say.

Right: You're considerate when it comes to calling, coming over, and making plans together.

Wrong: You promise to call and then don't see why you have to. You never let her know when you're coming, you just show up. You get furious when she makes her own plans because you haven't made any.

All of the "wrongs" can lead to becoming the kind of boy (and later, man) only girls who have a low opinion of themselves will date. Those bad habits may just overlap into your friendships as well. But all the "rights" can only take you in one direction — smooth relationships and good friendships.

To know if you are right or wrong, listen to what your girlfriend is trying to tell you.

Bobbie, 15, warned her boyfriend:

> "I said, 'Please don't call after 10 on school nights.' He kept right on doing it. It made my parents angry at him and at me. And it was a couple of other little things like that that made me stop liking him after a while."

Zina, 13, recalls, angrily:

> "Late. He was always late. I would wait for him 20 minutes. Sometimes a half hour. I got tired of it. And him, too."

Both of these girls ended up breaking up with their boyfriends because they were inconsiderate.

Or selfish. If going together can start in friendship, it will stay there. Being good friends with a girlfriend means you are open and honest and considerate. If you are, you will always be friends even when she's not your girlfriend.

CALLING IT QUITS

You're walking down the hall with a crushed piece of paper in your fist. You kick open your locker and get your books. Then you walk, fast, out of school. But before you leave, you stop at a wastebasket, take the piece of paper, tear it into little bits, and watch it drift to the bottom.

The girl you were going steady with broke up with you. And the way she did it. Crunch! Right in assembly with all the kids around. One by one they passed down a piece of paper. You started to read it and, at first, thought it was a joke. Some joke. You looked up to try and catch her eyes but she was staring, unblinking, at the stage. There you are holding a letter that says she doesn't want to go with you anymore. You feel like correcting the spelling errors and sending it back. After school you try to talk to her, but she's surrounded by her girlfriends and ignores you. She's called it quits. Just like that. With no warning.

Sometimes you don't understand girls at all. How can you turn off all the good feelings you had for her just because she doesn't like you anymore? Well, the way she broke up with you certainly helps, for starters.

Why Girls Do What They Do

Why would someone you see everyday and are used to talking with on the telephone every night write you a letter to break up? Abbie, 13, tells why:

> "Actually we didn't really break up when it was over. I just started getting sick of him. So I broke up with him. I wanted to go my own way. I wrote him a letter. I suppose I could have called him or told him, but I was really nervous about it."

Why was Abbie too nervous to talk to her boyfriend? She might have been afraid he would argue or try to talk her out of it. She was very afraid of saying what was on her mind and asserting herself. She also knew he would feel hurt and girls don't like to be hurtful, so she took the easy way out. She wrote him a letter. She probably slaved over every word, too. It's always better when you break up to tell the person. The trouble with writing a letter is that it's a one-sided conversation giving the other person no chance to answer you. Or to express important feelings.

Are you turning into an animal? If not, then why does a girl suddenly break up with you? Connie, 14, tells why:

> "He really didn't try anything. He was really nice and he didn't rush me. But it was just that I didn't feel comfortable at all. See, the three times I've been kissed by a boy, and I

don't mean a peck, it's not been fun at all. I never enjoyed it. I don't know what he was after, but he certainly wanted more than I wanted. My group of friends don't even really date, yet. Of course I had to break up with him."

Will a girl tell you how she feels when you get carried away with your feelings? Probably not. She's embarrassed and she's afraid. All she'll do is break up with you. Most boys learn to develop a kind of sixth sense and know when the girl doesn't feel the way they do. If this happens to you, don't turn an innocent mistake into an ugly ending. Talk over what has happened with your girlfriend.

What do you do when a girl is a little too honest? Some girls think honesty is the best policy. Beth, 13, tells why:

"I just told him honestly I wanted to break up. He was mad and he didn't think it was right, but after a while he cooled down. I felt better about it. I told him why. He said he understood."

It's not possible for a girl to be too honest. Beth had the courage to confront a boy who did disagree. She would have broken up with him anyway. It's kinder to break up honestly and openly. When you stop calling a girl or start ignoring her, the relationship doesn't have a real end to it.

It is better to be kind by saying something than suffer through this all-too familiar script many boys (and girls) will identify with.

Lucie, 14, tells her version:

"It was really strange. We just stopped calling each other. We both got kind of obnoxious on the phone and the calls got fewer and fewer and fewer and then it was over. I would have felt better if it was a nicer ending, but I just didn't want to deal with him.

How a Boy Can Call it Quits

1. **Do it in person.** If you're afraid she is going to cry and you can't stand the sight of tears, call her on the phone.

2. **Don't be cruel.** If you feel any anger, the temptation is to be downright nasty. If you break up simply, honestly, and briefly, though, you will be kind. Unless it's mutual, she is naturally going to feel hurt. You are telling her you don't want her anymore, and that might make her feel there is something wrong with her. That's the nature of rejection. There is nothing you can do about this except to assure her there is nothing wrong with *her*, but you both as a couple.

3. **Don't keep her waiting.** She may suspect that you no longer want to go steady anymore, but you won't talk about it. Rebecca, 14, had to go to a lot of trouble just to find out:

"He wouldn't tell me whether we were breaking up or not. So I went into the hall. He was with all the kids at the water fountain. I shouted, 'Are you breaking up with me or not?' He said, 'I'll call you.' Finally that night he called and said he liked me as a friend and nothing more. What I didn't like about it was he wouldn't tell me and wouldn't talk. I didn't just want to let it go. I wanted to know either way."

You might find yourself feeling a little jealous if she makes a quick recovery and you see her one day, laughing, joking, and having fun with the other boys. But it would be much worse if you didn't see her going out with other boys.

What To Do When She Breaks Up with You

Go on and admit that you feel hurt. You don't have to call up all your friends and sob, but at least be truthful to *yourself*. Many boys have a tendency to say, "Who me, hurt? You gotta be kidding. I never liked her anyway." It's not necessary to say anything like that to your friends. Never say it to yourself. Everyone feels something.

Put a lot of time into your favorite sport. This is called "letting off steam." It takes care of those angry, hurt, pent-up feelings for a while and gets them out of your system.

Don't withdraw and retreat back into a shell. Like a turtle, you may want to hide so you'll never see, hear, or have to take out a girl again. That's understandable. But go out with your boyfriends. Go out in a mixed group. Try going out with girls who are just friends. Mainly, go out and don't retreat.

Julie, 14, says:

> "I was dating the most popular guy in our school. He was president of his class and older. One day the girls in his class told him that he shouldn't be going with me. He needed a different type of girl. So he broke up with me. For three months I couldn't do anything, I felt so bad. Then one day I started to get angry. It seemed kind of stupid to waste my time with a boy like that who let other people tell him what to do and who to like. After that I started going out with my friends again."

Don't look for a replacement too soon. Too soon only means revenge on your old girlfriend. It might also mean the same thing could happen all over again. Take your time before you go steady again and when you do, take out a girl you not only like a lot but honestly think a lot of as a person.

Be brave and learn to live with rejection. Boys get more rejections than girls. They usually do most of the asking. Asking for a date and getting a "no" from a girl isn't so bad after a while. But if you ask her out and she rolls on the floor laughing, that can hurt. So can a girl's breaking up with you. But with time, it's not so bad.

Don't let yourself get too broken up over breaking up. You're not going to settle down at 12 or 14 (or even 16), so it would be logical to assume that you're going to do a lot of breaking up in the years to come. Many boys make up their minds, after a bad experience, that they'll never go steady again. No one is forcing you to go steady, but if you're afraid of getting too close to someone because you are actually afraid of getting hurt, admit it.

FRIENDS WHO ARE GIRLS

Boys and girls aren't so different. Think back to when you were in the first grade. You played with everyone and didn't even notice what sex they were. Then you got older and it began to make a difference. Your friends were boys. Girls stayed with girls.

It would be a mistake to have this attitude now. After a certain age, it makes a lot of sense for girls and boys to be friends. Girls make good friends. And they welcome the friendship of boys who are not boyfriends.

Laura, 13, thinks boyFRIENDS are great:

> "The boys in my class are all my friends. A year ago we didn't get along at all. Now I'm good friends with most of them."

Here are only a few reasons why this is true:

1. You feel free. You can say much more to a girlFRIEND than to your boy friends. Can you picture telling a boy friend, "I'm so shy when I'm around Susie, I start to stutter"? But you can tell this to a girl who is your friend. She'll understand and she'll probably say something helpful. Something that will make it easier for you to talk to Susie and relax more.

2. GirlFRIENDS are easy to be with. With a girlFRIEND, you'll find friendship comes naturally and you'll want to be with her.

3. Girls want you for a friend. It's helpful for a girl to have a boyFRIEND. She's eager and curious to know what boys are really like (just as you wonder what makes girls tick). She will think of you as a special friend.

Girls Talk About BoyFRIENDS

Bonnie, 15, who has good friends who are boys says:

> "They're practically the same as girlfriends. The boy I was just going out with is probably my best friend at this point. I have no trouble talking to him at all. But we don't date anymore and he's going out with someone else."

Denise, 12, couldn't agree more:

> "I know how boys feel when I'm friends with them and can talk to them. They're really like girls, you know that? They cover it up with other stuff."

They don't mean boys who are friends are unmasculine. They simply mean that when boys and girls meet on the same level, as friends, there's not that much difference. Sometimes they are surprised to find this is true. Boys and girls have the same problems, feel hurt or sad, get angry with other friends, and feel excited when someone they like likes them. But they look at it a little differently and that's what makes boy/girl friendships so interesting.

Most girls know how to get in touch with their emotions, recognize their feelings, and are not embarrassed to express them. But some boys have a tendency to run away from anything that might be deep or complicated to them. You can gain a lot from a girlFRIEND. You can listen to her talk. You can talk and she will listen. See if this true story seems typical to you:

Allison, 13, is going out with Jeffrey, also 13. They both have the same best friend. He's a boy. Allison can talk about Jeffrey anytime she wants to with this friend. *But*, Allison reports, it doesn't work the other way around. Jeffrey is also best friends with this boy and was before he started going with Allison. Can he also talk about Allison? "No, they don't," Allison says. "They don't really talk about things like that." Translation: Some boys talk only about sports or school or tell jokes with other boys. They can talk *about* girls but never about how they *feel* toward girls.

Some boys, of course, don't fit that stereotype at all. But others do find it hard to talk, really talk, about things that bother them with boy friends. GirlFRIENDS can come in very handy . . . if you talk to them.

Girls usually have a cluster of girlfriends to talk with for hours about everything. But girls who had problems said that they often went to their boyFRIENDS to talk these problems over.

Jacqui, 14, has a close boyFRIEND who gave her good advice:

"I was in a big, big, big fight with a couple of friends of mine. I was very upset and I didn't know if I was doing the right thing or the wrong thing or what. I asked my friend and he gave me advice. He told me to call up each friend and talk about it and be honest.

Sheri, 15, says she even takes problems that come up with girlfriends to her boyFRIENDS:

"A lot of people in my group are having problems with one girl who is very competitive. She has this attitude that she's above us all. Yet, she is our friend. She's in all my classes so I have to deal with her every day. It's hard. She makes silly comments about clothes, grades, and boys. She's someone we don't want to be around but she's always around. Instead of talking to her, we tend to talk behind her back. She cuts us down, too. Until I get up enough nerve and figure out how to tell her face to face what I think, it helps me to talk to the boys in my group."

BoyFRIENDS can be most useful to a girl when she doesn't know how to handle a real boyfriend. Girls like to know what boys think and are grateful for a boyFRIEND's advice. It's a very rewarding feeling to know you have helped a friend by giving advice. But advice can be very powerful. Have you ever noticed how some people pepper their conversation with phrases like "you should" or "you need to" or any sentence that begins with a verb and suggests someone do something. That's not the best way to give advice.

There's a much better way to give advice to your girlFRIEND. Listen to her. Try to relate any similar experiences you may have had. Give advice that's honest, thoughtful, and close to what you would do in her situation.

If you have girls as good friends, you might think this chapter is for another boy. Here are two reasons, though, not to skip over it:

First, can you honestly say you talk about what bothers you to your girlFRIENDS? Or do you just listen to their problems and play the role of big brother? If so, you're not taking advantage of the friendship. Your girlFRIEND might be able to be a better friend to you if you just give her the chance.

Ellie, 16, says:

> "Boys don't usually like to talk. Especially about their girlfriends. It's the other way around. They give me lots of advice. They do like to have girls as friends but they don't like to talk about anything that's bothering them."

Second, are you taking your girlFRIEND for granted? Not all boys are lucky enough to have girls for friends. Remember that she's a very special friend.

Rhonda, 12, says:

"There are boys who are my friends I can trust with my secrets. They help me with things. That's why I like them. If I liked any of them as real boyfriends, it would be all different. They would be friends but not the same kind of friends."

But what if you don't have a girlFRIEND? Get one — or more. Very funny, you're thinking. Because the girls in your class, if you even say hello, think you are trying to ask them out. Or they are so stuck-up they don't even know the boys are around. Maybe. Maybe not. It's not impossible to find a girlFRIEND. It may take opening your eyes and looking at girls in a different way, though.

How To Look for a GirlFRIEND
Look for a friend. Forget she's a girl.

Keep your eyes, ears, and mind open for any girl you can start a conversation with.

See if you like talking to her. Is she fun and your type of person?

Make sure she knows you want to be friends and you don't want to go out with her.

If she has a boyfriend, make sure he knows you don't want to go out with her.

If she's an old girlfriend, see if she wants to be a girlFRIEND.

It's not that hard to be friends with a girl once you find one you want to be friends with — and who wants to be friends with you.

Carrie, 14, likes having boys for friends:

"The majority of my good friends happen to
be boys. It's really good to be able to talk to
them."

There is a special way to treat a girlFRIEND,
though. It's nice to know, even if you already
have one.

1. **Communicate.** Talk about everything. If
there's a misunderstanding or one of you gets
angry, mention it and talk about it. Then drop it.

2. **Trust her.** Forget about all those old-
fashioned jokes and programs you might see on
TV. You know the kind — girls are emotional,
brainless, blabby. Or girls don't make good
friends. Judge your girlFRIEND by her own
merits. Is she your good friend or not?

3. **Talk about yourself.** That's what friendship
is all about. You talk . . . she listens . . . you listen
. . . she talks. If you've never talked about yourself, your feelings, secrets, and goals — try it!
You can even talk about your girlfriend. Because you trust your girlFRIEND.

There is a problem that happens sometimes
with girlFRIEND/boyFRIEND relationships. It
can totally destroy the friendship almost overnight. It happens when one of you begins to
think of your special friend not just as a friend,
but someone *very* special. Romantic thoughts
come creeping into your mind suddenly. But you
know the truth is that this has been building all
along. It's wonderful and natural when two good

friends decide they want to become a couple. It's not so great when only one of three friends comes to this decision.

Here's what happened to Enid, 14:

> "I like boys for friends. It really helps, you know? Especially if you're having problems with someone and you feel like talking. But it backfires sometimes. That's what happened to me with this boy I was friends with last year. I had been discussing another guy with him, which wasn't anything out of the ordinary. He started to get very upset. I asked him why and he said that *he* liked me. I felt awful. I thought I might actually be able to do something to stop him from liking me. I wanted him for a friend. For about two or three weeks, I felt really uncomfortable. Finally I went up to him and said, 'Look, we're good friends. We'll always be good friends. But I just can't see it turning into anything more.'"

Remember the first rule for being friends with a girl? Communicate. If you find yourself liking, really liking, a girlFRIEND, tell her right away. Taking her by surprise or assuming she feels the same way you do will do nothing for your friendship. It might even end it. If she doesn't feel the same way you do, she'll be angry, confused, and frightened. She won't want to lose you as a friend. Also, if you notice your girlFRIEND acting differently, find out if she likes *you* as more than a friend. The best way is to discuss it.

Girls and boys are the same . . . but different. You'll find many girls who think like you, feel about things the same way you do, and don't seem too different. But they *are* different in the way they approach things. It's that difference that makes girlFRIENDS valuable friends to have. It's also the reason girls want to have you for a boyFRIEND.

Some of these things will make you feel uneasy and maybe a little angry. You'll want to defend yourself. But that's not the point. If you feel the girls are criticizing you, think of it as criticism that can help you. Constructive criticism. Maybe what girls have to say will teach you something about yourself. Then you'll be able to handle your relationships and friendships better. That's all that's important. If you keep an open mind, you might just learn how to get along better with girls.

Josie, 14, gets impatient with boys who don't listen:

> "Sometimes when they get nervous, they say things I think are really dumb when I'm trying to have an important conversation with them. They start making stupid jokes. That always bothers me. Everything will be normal and they'll start acting like that just because I want to talk about something. I think they don't like it, so they act silly so they don't have to hear what you're saying. They don't listen. They change the subject."

If you act this way when a girl is trying to tell you something she thinks is important, it's because you are anxious. You are afraid to find out what it is. It's obvious she's got her whole speech planned and it's going to be a heavy one. It's easier to run away by interrupting her, telling jokes, or trying to change the subject. But it won't work. If she has something to tell you, you're going to hear it sooner or later. You will just make matters worse and her angrier by putting it off.

Helpful hint: Try instead to tell yourself this: "Oh, no, here it comes. I feel nervous." Then be quiet and let her talk. Something is surely bothering her or something is important to her. You would like her to listen to you. If you give her this chance to speak her mind, you will probably find it is easier to handle whatever it is she has to tell you.

Joanie, 16, does not like boys who try *too* hard:

> "I don't like it when boys ask personal questions and we don't even know each other very well. One boy asked if I liked him or not and why not and I was forced to start explaining. It was out of the blue. It was pretty embarrassing. Another thing I don't like are boys who play very easy to get. They're just right there at your feet and they almost have a sign on them, "Here I am!" I like a boy who likes me but doesn't let me know *that* much that he likes me. A girl can tell, anyway. I like things to be more subtle. Even if I liked a boy a lot I wouldn't want him to act that way. I would think there was something wrong."

Being assertive or knowing what you want and going after it is a positive, good quality in a boy or girl. But when the opposite sex is involved it gets a little more complicated. It is not advisable to go around acting like Mr. Cool or a teenage television idol. But the exact opposite, Mr. Uncool, is just as bad. If you are always following a girl around demanding to know how much she likes you and you act jealous and possessive, it tells the girl something very important about you. It says you are unsure of yourself. You are not confident enough to believe anyone would like you and you are going to cause her problems.

Helpful hint: This is the one time to "cool" it. The more independent you can act (and that doesn't mean playing games or taking out other girls behind her back), the more she will think you're a confident, secure person. Let her know you like her but don't knock her over the head with it every minute. Look up the word "subtle" in your dictionary. Read all the meanings. Put this word into practice when it comes to your relationships with girls. Keep in mind that girls don't like to be pushed or pressured by boys. It turns them off.

Wendy, 13, thinks boys are *too* close to their same-sex friends:

> "They're not open and they seem very afraid of girls. Because they want so much to have same-sex friends. I think the reason the girls get so disgusted with the boys is that they seem to act so disgusted around girls.

Our club, when we have a baseball game, would be a lot more willing to let the boys in than they would be to let us in. Boys really group together."

Oh, very funny, you're probably thinking. And girls don't group together? With their clothes and slumber parties and confidences. You're right, of course, but you also see that they think boys group together too much. So much so that girls can't break through that barrier because boys make it impossible.

Helpful hint: The next time your crowd has a game, let the girls play. It would be a different kind of game than the one you usually play. Do play to win but relax and have some fun with the game. You just might find a girl who's just as good a ballplayer as you. Boys group together because it's safe and comfortable. Don't be afraid to un-group a little. It's very hard to get to know girls if you don't.

Rebecca, 12, likes a boy who's leaving her with black-and-blue marks:

"I like him and I know he likes me. But he keeps banging me on the back. Or punching me. I know he's hitting me because he likes me and I really like him, but sometimes it hurts."

Rebecca's boyfriend is suffering from a symptom of being caught in the middle of growing up. It's called "King Kong"-itis. It means he does like her a lot but shows his affection by using her as a human punching bag, because that's how he's used to relating to his boyfriends. They wrestle and punch and pound and everyone knows they are loved. Another reason boys become miniature King Kongs when they are with a girl they like is simply because they're nervous. Girls don't like this very much.

Helpful hint: Think before you raise your hitting arm. Smile and say, "Hi, what's new?" or anything at the time that feels natural to you. Soon talking and smiling and laughing with the girl you like will come easier than beating her up.

Susan, 13, complains about boys who are afraid to talk to girls because their boy friends might not approve:

> "Boys are so incapable of having relationships with girls. All they want to do is wrestle with each other it seems. Not one of them has the guts to do something different. There's this group. I don't like them. If just one boy from that group sits next to me in school, his group will immediately start to tease us."

Peer pressure. Boys have it. Girls have it. Even adults have it. You know how they are — the house has to be just right, the car has to stand out, and even the children have to be better than all their friends' children. Yet, the kind of peer pressure your parents are up against isn't really half as bad as the peer pressure you face now. It is very, very difficult for a boy to break away from his good boyfriends and get to know a girl better. But it is far from impossible.

Helpful hint: If you have peer pressure from your boyfriends, remember that every single boy in that group is weak. That's right. Only when a boy gets into a group does he feel strong. But it's the group that has the power, not each boy in it. If just one boy leaves the group and shows an interest in a girl, the whole group is threatened. The same thing might happen again and again to the other boys. With no boys, there goes the group and the power. Your boy friends might not consciously realize it's to their advantage to keep you in your place (away from girls), but that is what their actions say every time you show an interest in a girl. It's a strong boy who can say to his friends, "I'm going with her." You have to realize that the group, one day, will break apart. This is because you will all change and grow and be entirely different. *You* may have already started growing. All you need is the courage to go your own way.

Girls Talk About Love

Girls think about love often and what it means to them. They would really rather do that than criticize or gossip about boys. Have you ever wondered what girls thought love was? They'll tell you.

Missy, 14:

"I always think about it. I think love is wanting to be with a boy and talk with him and just be together all the time."

Christine, 15:

"I'd say it's kind of a mutual caring for each other and an honest relationship. One where petty arguments don't get in the way. What love is about really depends on the people."

Sandra, 12:

"Oh, boy. Two people meeting each other and liking each other a lot. Then it grows into love."

Jessica, 15:

"I guess love is having special feelings about someone, caring for someone, and having a special relationship. One that's intimate, honest, and comfortable."

Elizabeth, 14:

"Love is when you lose your appetite."

Love is all that to girls. Some girls said they didn't know exactly what it was because they had never experienced it yet, but were looking forward to it.

Girls, basically, feel the same way as boys do about love. There's the love you feel for your parents, your friends, and your pets. Then there's that certain someone that you feel, or know you're going to feel, just a little more special toward.

There's another kind of love that is a prerequisite to loving someone else. A prerequisite is the same thing as having to take algebra before you can take geometry. You have to know one first to move to the other well.

To love, you have to love *yourself* first. That means looking beyond the pimples, what the other boys do, all the things you think you never fail to mess up, and looking into yourself. What's the real boy like in there? If you met that guy at a party or in school, would you want to be friends with him?

Stephanie, 13, has this thought:

> "All love is to me, at my age, is the going out with a boy and having a friendship. Even if you split up with him the next day, you always have a friendship. If you don't, you're not friends with yourself."

119